D0436886

Mark Skousen's
Thirty-Day Plan to Financial Independence

OTHER BOOKS BY MARK SKOUSEN

Playing the Price Controls Game

The Insider's Banking & Credit Almanac

High Finance on a Low Budget (co-authored with Jo Ann Skousen)

The Complete Guide to Financial Privacy

Tax Free

The Structure of Production

Economics on Trial

Scrooge Investing

Dissent on Keynes (editor)

The Investor's Bible

Mark Skousen's
Thirty-Day Plan to Financial Independence

Mark Skousen
Editor, *Forecasts & Strategies*

Regnery Publishing
Washington, D.C.

Copyright © 1995 by Mark Skousen

All rights reserved. No part of this publication may be reproduced or transmitted in any form or by any means electronic or mechanical, including photocopy, recording, or any information storage and retrieval system now known or to be invented, without permission in writing from the publisher, except by a reviewer who wishes to quote brief passages in connection with a review written for inclusion in a magazine, newspaper, or broadcast.

Library of Congress Cataloging-in-Publication Data

Skousen, Mark.
    [Thirty day plan to financial independence]
    Mark Skousen's thirty day plan to financial independence
        p.   cm.
    Includes index.
    ISBN 0-89526-478-1
    1. Finance, Personal. I. Title. II. Title: Thirty day plan to
financial independence.
HG179.S5283 1995
332.024—dc20   94-45415
                                                     CIP

Published in the United States by
Regnery Publishing, Inc.
An Eagle Publishing Company
422 First Street, S.E., Suite 300
Washington, DC 20003

Distributed to the trade by
National Book Network
4720-A Boston Way
Lanham, MD 20706

Printed on acid-free paper.
Manufactured in the United States of America

10 9 8 7 6 5 4 3 2 1

Books are available in quantity for promotional or premium use. Write to Director of Special Sales, Regnery Publishing, Inc., 422 First Street, SE, Suite 300, Washington, DC 20003, for information on discounts and terms or call (202) 546-5005.

To Jo Ann,
My co-author in the book of life

"Economy is in itself a source of great revenue."
—Seneca

"To resist change is like holding your breath—if you persist, you will die."
—Lao Tsu

CONTENTS

THIRD WEEK: Increase Your Income and Investments

FOURTH WEEK: Build Your Net Worth

FIFTH WEEK: Go on Automatic Pilot

ACKNOWLEDGMENTS

There's something exciting about the prospect of achieving your goals in just thirty days—one month from now. Thirty days to thin thighs...Thirty days to a muscular body...Thirty days to stop smoking...Thirty days to a happy marriage...We all want to get our house in order and enjoy life to the fullest. Well, then, why not thirty days to financial independence?

I used the "thirty day" principle in writing this book. A chapter a day for thirty days and, voila! the guidebook is complete. Actually, of course, writing this book required a lot more than just thirty days. In many ways, it represents a lifetime of work. In my case, twenty years in the financial world helped me prepare to write this book.

My indebtedness goes to many people. First, I'd like to thank Karim Rahemtulla, financial editor of Taipan and research director at Agora in Baltimore. Karim is a gifted researcher, writer, and philosopher who contributed immensely to the middle chapters in the book.

I also would like to thank my wife, Jo Ann, who is currently a fellow in English at Rollins College in Winter Park, Florida. She spent many hours religiously editing every chapter, adding much new material, and correcting many misconceptions. Many of the stories and insights contained in this work are hers. Without her efforts, this book would not be published today.

I also express appreciation to the following individuals: Gary Alexander, Debora Corral, Jon Golding, Harry Browne, Stephanie Gallagher, Bob and Janet Kephart, Dave Phillips, Richard Band, Adrian Day, John Schaub, and John Templeton.

Mark Skousen
Winter Park, Florida

HERE'S WHAT YOU WILL
ACCOMPLISH IN THIRTY DAYS

1. You will be on the road to financial independence.

2. You will start a money machine that will generate untold wealth automatically and painlessly.

3. You will create the Automatic Wealth Builder, an investment account that never stops growing.

4. You will develop a great new source of liquid cash—to buy a home, start your own business, pay for your children's education, or go on the vacation of a lifetime.

5. You will tap into the most successful businesses around the world.

6. You will adopt a simple, powerful, technique that automatically reduces and eventually eliminates all your consumer debts.

7. You will eliminate wasteful spending habits while increasing your standard of living.

8. You will discover the secret of becoming wealthier every month no matter how much you spend.

9. You will begin a physical improvement program that will increase your wealth and make you feel better.

10. You will reduce your tax burden, giving you more money to spend and invest.

11. You will discover the best ways to raise cash instantly, in a matter of days.

12. You will learn a simple, easy way to get a 10 percent raise at work.

13. You will learn how to make "lady luck" work for you, year in and year out.

14. You will find out how to obtain the best financial information for free.

15. You will create a living will and adopt other "estate planning" tools that will protect you and your estate from taxes and lawsuits.

Welcome to Mark Skousen's Thirty-Day Plan to Financial Independence.

CAN YOU KEEP A SECRET?

A group of visitors called upon a famous wealthy man, anxious to learn how he had become financially independent. As the group was ushered into the great hall to meet this well-to-do figure, one of the visitors stepped forward and asked, "Sir, tell us how you became so wealthy, while the rest of us remain so poor?"

The rich man smiled and said, "I'll tell you my little secret to success on one condition—you must promise never to tell another soul." They all nodded their heads. Then, in a solemn whisper, he said, "I make money while I sleep!" The crowd of listeners looked perplexed, so the millionaire explained.

"All of you work hard for a living and make money during the day, do you not?" They all agreed. "But the secret to financial independence," said the sage, "is to make money while you are asleep."

"But how can we make money while we're asleep—that's impossible," a skeptical visitor muttered.

"It's very simple," said the rich man. "You must search and find someone who will pay you while you sleep! All of you are used to paying others for the things you want in life. Now all you have to do is go out and find someone willing to pay you!"

"But, sir, we don't know anyone like that," said another visitor. "What sane person would do such a foolish thing?"

"You are right," continued the wealthy citizen. "Most people won't. Certainly your boss won't pay you while you sleep. Neither will most of your friends. But, fortunately, there are a few persons who will gladly do so."

"Who? Who?" the audience demanded impatiently.

"Well," the millionaire said, "there's my banker downtown. He pays me interest while I sleep. There's the president of the local utility company. He pays me dividends while I sleep. There are my tenants. They pay me rent while I sleep. There's the president of a manufacturing firm. He pays me capital gains while I sleep. Why, every month, just like clockwork, I receive several checks in the mail from these sources, a considerable sum of money. In fact, I receive so much money each month that I no longer have to work for a living."

"And you did nothing in return?"

"That's right. I didn't work one minute for any of them. All I did was lend them some of my surplus wealth, and they pay me for the privilege of using my money. I am therefore making money all the time, not just during the day."

"How can we do that, too?"

"It's very simple," said the rich man. "All you need to do is lend these institutions some of your hard-earned savings, and it won't be long before you too will be making money while you sleep. You can be just like me and get a monthly check without fail and be on the road to financial independence."

Then, in closing, he gave one word of warning: "But, remember, if you spend all your income, or go into debt, you won't have any money to lend or invest. You'll never receive those monthly checks, and you'll never make money while you sleep. You'll work all day and have nothing to show for it. If you want to be financially independent like me, you have to retain surplus wealth and put it to profitable use."

INTRODUCTION

Thirty days to financial independence?

When I mentioned the title of this new book to a friend, he looked incredulous. "You can't be serious! Nobody gets rich in thirty days. It takes years, maybe a lifetime—if you're lucky."

Then he looked me straight in the eye, anxious to know my formula. "How is it possible?"

"Simple," I replied. "You mentioned the right word—luck. On Day 1, you buy a Florida lottery ticket. On Day 2, you buy two Florida lottery tickets...."

Now he knew I was kidding!

But, gentle reader, the title of this book is not so ridiculous as it may seem. By following the simple, easy-to-understand steps presented in this book, by the end of thirty days you will be on the road to financial independence. You will be able to make money while you sleep. It will no longer be a question of *if* you become independently wealthy. It will only be a question of *when* you have all the money you want in life.

This guidebook is not about winning the lottery, inheriting a fortune, or how to parlay a million dollars in thirty days at the craps table in Las Vegas. My formula doesn't depend on luck. It is a systematic approach that virtually guarantees your financial success, no matter who you are. My program works for people in all walks of life, whether earning a high income or low income. It works for teachers, construction workers, secretaries, accountants, pastors, salesmen, store clerks, or presidents of corporations. It even works for lawyers (unfortunately).

Heavily in debt and can't make ends meet? You will be on the road to success within thirty days. Just follow the day-by-day steps. It's that simple.

The exciting thing about my system is that, once in place, everything takes care of itself automatically. This is the genius of this program. This isn't one of those programs that requires you to spend thirty minutes each day for the rest of your life. Rather, it is a system that requires only thirty days of preparation. Once you have established the system, no further work is required. You can go about your business as usual, having the peace of mind that comes from knowing your financial affairs are all taken care of. That's quite a blessing in today's uncertain world.

It's what fellow investment advisor Richard Band calls "The Law of Inevitable Wealth." Follow it, and you will inevitably be rich.

The Investment Account That Never Stops Growing

Thousands of people have followed my thirty-day plan, have gotten out of debt, and are building wealth rapidly.

Take my own case, for example. No, this is not a story of how I was on my last penny and miraculously became wealthy overnight. I was doing fine, but I wanted to do better. So in March 1993, I opened a special investment account with $5,000. I called it "The Investment Account That Never Stops Growing." I signed the papers for this account and have done absolutely nothing more. I just sit and watch it grow. I pay no commissions whatsoever for this account. I receive a monthly statement indicating how much my account is worth. Guess what? A year later, March 1994, the account reached $18,000. By December, as I write this introduction, it's worth over $28,000.

As you can see, it's growing very rapidly. If you follow my plan, it won't be long before you too will be financially independent. It's only a matter of time until you will be making money while you sleep. And the sooner the better!

Build an Independent Source of Wealth

The purpose of this guidebook is to show you how to build an independent source of wealth—independent of your salary or wage, independent of your retirement program, and independent of Social Security and other government programs. In today's world of deficit spending, inflation, and downsizing, you can't always count on traditional sources of income anymore.

The independent source of wealth you will be creating is money that you can use at any time without restriction. Use it now or at any time to enjoy life—buy a home, start a new business, go on a trip, buy a new car, take college courses, or enjoy dance lessons. The choices are endless. And they are all within your grasp in just thirty days. How much independence you achieve is completely up to you... not your boss, your relatives, nor the government. You decide how wealthy you want to be.

Change Your Mind-Set

In order for my thirty-day plan to work, you have to change your mind-set. For the next thirty days, I want you to think and act very differently from the way you've been doing. During the next month, I want you to think about selling rather than buying. I want you to forget about spending and concentrate on saving. I want you to think about raising cash instead of buying on credit. Instead of going into debt, I want you think of getting out of debt. Instead of going to a garage sale and picking up some bargains, I want you to plan on selling and raising cash at your own garage sale.

For many of you, this may be a whole new way of behavior. But don't worry. Think of it as a fun, new way of living. There really isn't a lot of work involved. In fact, each day requires you to spend only about an hour or two of your time. The thirty-day plan demands little time or effort for tremendous results, but you must be willing to concentrate.

What This Book Is All About

This guidebook is divided into thirty chapters, each chapter indicating what you need to do each day for the next thirty days. Each day's activities are presented in a logical sequence.

The first week's activities (Days 1-7) involve setting up the Automatic Wealth Builder that is central to the whole system of achieving financial independence. It will show you how to build wealth quickly and painlessly, without taking much risk. You will learn the secret of building wealth every month no matter how much you spend.

The second week's activities (Days 8-14) focus on the expenditure side of your finances. Once you put in place the Automatic Wealth Builder, it will undoubtedly put pressure on your budget, requiring you to watch your expenses more closely. But I have developed a simple, easy way to control your spending without creating a formal budget. I call it the "Financial Freedom" Budget. It will show you how to cut your cost of living without cutting your standard of living.

The third week's activities (Days 15-21) focus on the income side of your finances. I demonstrate proven ways to obtain a raise, increase your income, find a better job, and even start your own business. (Your Automatic Wealth Builder will provide the "seed capital" you'll need to get started!) You can achieve independent wealth much more quickly if you earn more income. Days 15-21 will show you the way.

The fourth week's activities (Days 22-28) discuss problems of debt, credit cards, and bankruptcy. If you face financial difficulties, these chapters are for you. They will show you how to gain control of your financial life without filing for bankruptcy (your last resort). You may be surprised to discover how many people with grave financial woes have turned their lives around within thirty days by using the techniques discussed in Days 22-28.

The fifth week's activities (Days 29-30) are short, but involve a positive review of all the concepts, and how you can increase your net worth rapidly.

Each week also includes a day of meditation, when you can reflect upon your achievements of the previous days and prepare for the goals of the coming week. Don't shortchange yourself. Most people need to take more time to think and ponder what they are doing in life and where they are headed.

Well, that covers the overall picture. Let's not waste another moment. Get started with Day 1.

FIRST WEEK:
Start Your Automatic Investment Plan Now

TAKE A "WEALTH BUILDING" VACATION
Set Your Goals

"What do you do for a living?"

The question came from a stern-looking customs agent as I entered the United States from a trip abroad.

I said simply, "I'm independently wealthy."

It was not the right thing to say. The customs agent didn't believe a young fellow in his thirties could be financially independent. He started asking a lot of questions. I think he was envious.

Independently wealthy. It has a certain ring to it, doesn't it? A ring of ultimate success. You have finally made it in life, at least monetarily. You have reached the lofty position of not having to work for a living if you so choose—of having enough money in the bank to live off the interest and do what you please.

Financial independence means having an "independent" means of support—independent of your full-time work. This doesn't mean that once you achieve financial independence you will quit work altogether and live off your investment income. You might be able to do that someday, but I doubt if you would want to. "Retirement" can be unfulfilling, unrewarding, and deadly. Even the wealthiest people are usually engaged in a variety of pursuits. It's important that you keep working and doing the things you enjoy in life. The point is that financial independence means you don't have to work.

Your First Step

The first step to financial independence is the easiest, but you may be tempted not to do it. Here's what I want you to do: Take a one-day vacation and meditate on what you are about to achieve over the next thirty days.

Yes, that's right, take the day off. If you have a full-time job, take vacation leave or sick leave. If that's not possible, plan on taking a one-day vacation on Saturday or Sunday. Don't just sit at home and read this book. Get away from your usual pursuits and go to a relaxed location where you won't be bothered by daily routines, business, family problems, or other distractions.

Consider:

- ◆ going to the beach
- ◆ going camping
- ◆ traveling to your favorite resort
- ◆ going to a park

Just remember: Take this guidebook with you, and plan your strategy for financial success. I guarantee that you will never be the same.

My "first day" activity may seem unnecessary to you, but it is critical to your financial well-being. If you don't have the right frame of mind, you probably won't achieve the monetary goals you desire.

How Much Does It Take to Be Independently Wealthy?

What are you trying to achieve?

How much money do you need to be financially independent? A million dollars in net assets? Two million? Three million?

It all depends on your lifestyle. If you had a million dollars, and you put that million dollars into an investment paying 10 percent each year, you would have $100,000 a year to live on. Is that enough? Perhaps, perhaps not. I have met people from all walks of life and lifestyles, and their financial requirements vary considerably. Some people need very little to enjoy life, while others demand substantially more. Decide for yourself how much money you need to enjoy life and do the things you want to do.

The first thing we want to do on Day 1 is figure out how much money you need to live comfortably.

Start with monthly income. Figure out how much monthly income you need to enjoy life and do the things you want to do. Be generous. How much would you need every month for housing, transportation, clothing, food, entertainment, and, oh yes, don't forget taxes? Add it all up and write that figure down in the space below.

HOW MUCH MONEY YOU NEED TO LIVE COMFORTABLY

Monthy income needed _____

   Now multiply that monthly figure by twelve, which will equal the yearly income you will need.

Yearly income needed ___ _____

   Finally, multiply that yearly figure by ten, which will give you the total investment capital you will need to generate that much monthly income.

Total investment capital needed _____

This amount will tell you how much you need in liquid assets which, if invested at a 10 percent annual rate of return, would give you the monthly income required to be financially independent.

This last figure, your total investment capital, represents your GOAL. It may seem like an impossible number to achieve, but believe me, after following the techniques described in this book, you will be on your way in no time.

Pretty simple for Day 1, isn't it?

The rest is just as easy. On to Day 2!

ACTIONS TO TAKE ON DAY 1

1. Take a one-day "wealth building" vacation—someplace where you can relax and think, away from home and job.

2. Use my simple formula to determine how much capital you need to become financially independent.

3. Congratulate yourself for taking the first step on the road to financial freedom.

CALL THIS TOLL-FREE NUMBER
And Be on the Road to Financial Success

On Day 2, you have it made. All you need to do is call this toll-free number: 800-526-8600.

But before you call, read this chapter. You are calling Charles Schwab & Co., the nationwide discount brokerage firm. You will ask for two items:

♦ First, an account opening application, and

♦ Second, an application for Schwab's Automatic Investment Plan (AIP).

If Schwab has a local office, stop by and pick up these applications in person.

Why Schwab? No, I'm not on commission. I'm recommending Schwab's AIP because it is the first and most important step on your road to financial independence. Schwab's AIP is convenient, flexible, and, most important, commission free.

Two Alternative Sources

If you would like some alternatives, here are two other nation-wide discount brokerage firms that offer similar plans:

♦ Fidelity Funds Network, P.O. Box 660306, Dallas, Texas 75266, 800-544-9697. The Fidelity family of funds has discount brokerage offices around the country and is similar to Schwab in commission rates. Currently, it offers over three hundred no-load mutual funds.

♦ Jack White & Co., 9191 Towne Centre Drive, Suite 220, San Diego, California 92122, 800-233-3411. Based in San Diego, this discount brokerage firm offers a program similar to Schwab's. *Smart Money* recently rated it the top-rated discount broker firm in the nation for its services and prices. Jack White is licensed in all fifty states.

The Advantages of Automatic Investing

Schwab's AIP (as well as Fidelity's and Jack White's) makes it easy for you to build wealth automatically and painlessly. Here's how it works. When you receive your application, fill it out. You decide how much money you wish to invest each month (or quarter). Arrange to have this amount of money withdrawn automatically each month (or quarter) from your paycheck or checking account. Schwab makes all the arrangements for you with your bank or place of employment.

Finally, decide what kind of investments you wish to make.

Schwab has over two hundred no-load mutual funds to choose from. You have the choice of investing in growth stocks, blue-chip companies, income investments, foreign markets, and gold. The decision is completely up to you. In the next several days, we will help you decide which investments you wish to make.

Schwab's AIP is the special investment account I wrote about in the introduction—"The Investment Account That Never Stops Growing."

Saving and investing become a lot more interesting and exciting when you know you're piling up money fast every month.

So call Schwab at 800-526-8600, or visit a local office, and get started today building an independent source of wealth.

Then move on to Day 3 to find out why this Automatic Wealth Builder is the easiest and fastest way to financial success.

ACTIONS TO TAKE ON DAY 2

Take the most important step of all. Call one of my recommended brokerage firms (Schwab, Fidelity, or Jack White) and ask for an application to open an account and an Automatic Investment Plan (AIP).

DAY

3

REWARD YOURSELF:
Part of All You Earn Is
Yours to Keep

Day 3 is easy. All you have to do is read this chapter and understand why the Automatic Wealth Builder, discussed in Day 2, is absolutely essential for financial independence. Once you catch the vision of how powerful this technique is, you will get as excited as I am about building wealth automatically.

Let me start by telling you a true story. Several years ago a medical doctor called me to ask for a consultation. He said that he was an extremely successful physician in New York City, making half a million dollars a year, but he just couldn't make ends meet. He said he wanted to meet with me personally and would spend whatever time—even several days if necessary—to solve his financial woes. I told him that I didn't need to meet with him for several days—one hour would be sufficient.

"Should I bring my tax returns and net worth statement?" he asked.

"No, I won't need them."

He seemed incredulous, but decided to meet with me anyway. When he arrived at my office, he started in on his troubles. He complained about the high cost of living in Manhattan, the cost of hiring good help, the exorbitant tax rates in the city, his wife's spending habits, and a host of other expenses that left him with nothing but debts at the end of each year. I began to feel sorry for a fellow earning half a million a year!

Finally, I spoke up. "You know what your problem is? You pay everyone else before you pay yourself." He didn't understand.

"Look," I said, "you're paying everyone on time—your assistants, bookkeeper, landlord, suppliers, the IRS, the City of New York, and your wife. But you never get around to paying yourself. Nothing is left over for you!"

He got the point. Then I suggested a simple solution to his problem. "Instruct your bookkeeper to set aside $2,000 at the beginning of each month and put it in a money market fund. Make sure she puts aside this amount at the first of the month before paying any other bills. Do it without fail, no matter what other bills are pending."

The doctor was very skeptical because he was already spending everything he earned. "That's it? You have no other suggestions, such as where to cut back on my expenses, how to live within a budget, or how to increase my income?"

"No. None whatsoever."

The doctor had a look of total disbelief as I escorted him out of my office, but he had agreed to try it. The hour was up.

A year later, the doctor called me on the telephone. His voice was gruff and contentious. "Mr. Skousen, I just want you to know that my financial woes are just as bad as a year ago. Taxes in the city have skyrocketed, my costs have risen, and I had to hire another assistant. My wife is still spending money like crazy on Fifth Avenue. I still have a devil of a time making ends meet. It's like I'm digging a hole that gets deeper and deeper every year." Then there was a pause. "Nothing has changed, Mr. Skousen... except for one thing."

"What's that?" I asked.

"I have over $24,000 in a money market fund. What should I do with it?"

Amazing, isn't it?

Why did my advice work? Because making, spending, and investing money is all in the mind. The good doctor followed a simple plan that relied on the psychological truth: "Money you don't see you don't spend." By having his bookkeeper remove $2,000 on the first of each month, the doctor didn't notice the money and didn't spend it. I figured that with half a million dollars coming into his practice each year, he was surely wasting at least $2,000 a month on things he never really wanted or needed. To this day I have no idea what he was wasting his money on, and neither has he. But the funny thing is that by removing $2,000 each month automatically from his business account, he was forced to cut back somewhere, somehow, and to live within a slightly, almost unnoticeably, lower budget. And it worked.

Notice, also, that the doctor was able to accumulate $24,000 in investment funds without relying on a tight budget plan or developing ways to earn more money. A budget and income plan may be useful, but it isn't necessary to make this system work.

Why Most Budgets Don't Work

Budgeting doesn't usually work for long. It's like dieting. A new thirty-day diet plan works for thirty days, and then you go back to your old eating habits. Budgets often don't work because unexpected emergencies come up and destroy your plans. Or your determination breaks down and you give up. With an Automatic

Investment Plan (AIP), you accumulate a large independent source of wealth very quickly without relying on strict budgets or new sources of income. And you can start today.

Is Your Saving Plan Easy or Difficult?

Too many earners make it difficult to save and easy to spend. Suppose you want to start saving some money for a future goal— a summer vacation, a house or a car, or a new business. You decide to save $100 each paycheck. If you get paid once every two weeks, you theoretically will save $2,600 in one year, a sizable amount. But I can tell you right now that you won't achieve your goal. At some point during the year, an emergency or unexpected expense will come up, and you'll discontinue your plan to set aside $100 every two weeks in savings. The car will break down, someone in the family will get sick, you'll need a new appliance, you'll have to go to a funeral, and so on. The list is endless. You can always count on unexpected expenditures!

The fact is, you have made it difficult to save. If you get paid once every two weeks, you have to make a decision—yes or no— whether to save twenty-six times a year!

Why not use a system that makes it easy to save, the one that requires you to make only one decision? Everything else is taken care of.

The IRS Knows the Secret

Believe it or not, the federal government is an excellent example of how to accumulate wealth the easy way. It's called withholding. Every paycheck, Uncle Sam removes a huge percentage (as much as 39.6 percent, plus Social Security and other taxes) automatically from your wage or salary. Imagine what it would be like if you had to pay one lump payment of federal income tax on April 15th! Very few could afford it. There would be a tax rebellion (not a bad idea!). But the IRS cleverly avoids a tax rebellion by taking out a relatively small amount of funds each paycheck. Whoever invented tax withholding was a genius. (I hear it was free-market economist Milton Friedman!) It started during World War II as a temporary "emergency" measure and has escalated to today's nearly confiscatory rates.

Why not use the same technique the IRS uses to confiscate your hard-earned money? Only in your case, you'll be using it to build a fortune for you.

If you want to solve your financial problems, imitate the IRS! Have a certain percentage of your wage or salary taken out of your paycheck (or checking account), and have it invested automatically in your favorite investments.

Automatic Investment Plans

There are many AIPs to choose from.

◆ *Payroll Deductions*—Your company may offer several choices, such as U.S. savings bonds, credit union savings accounts, company stock purchase plans, or mutual funds. Your company's financial benefits officer can explain each of these programs for you, including details of specific funds and company matching programs that may exist. Most choices are pretty limited, so before you sign up for these plans, consider the Automatic Wealth Building Plan I've developed in Day 2 (the AIP offered by Schwab, Fidelity, and Jack White). Even if you do have one of these payroll deduction plans, you still need an AIP.

◆ *Pension Plans*—What about 401(k) and other company-sponsored retirement plans? I'm all for them. This is a great way to build wealth automatically. A certain percentage of your income is deducted each pay period and invested in various mutual funds. You pay no tax on your investments while inside the pension plan, and your contributions are tax deductible. A great way to accumulate wealth tax-free! Be sure to diversify into a variety of investment choices. If your 401(k) plan or profit-sharing plan offers international stocks and bonds, take advantage of them. If your company doesn't offer this option, suggest that they add such funds. Remember, we live in a global economy.

♦ *Investment Clubs*—Investment clubs follow the principles of automatic wealth building. Like-minded investors get together once a month, make regular deposits, choose individual stocks, and invest in them. They live by three grand principles:

1. invest regularly

2. buy growth stocks

3. reinvest all dividends

Investment clubs can be a great way to build wealth painlessly and easily. The National Association of Investment Clubs tells the story of a man who joined a club, investing only $20 a month, and finally retired after thirty years with $105,000! Now that's the closest thing to getting something for nothing that I know. It certainly is far better than the chance of hitting it big playing the Florida lottery or the jackpot at Caesar's Palace!

Gambling Is No Way to Get Rich

Speaking of gambling, recently I overheard a Florida man talking about his own unique "investment" plan. He "invests" $100 a week in the Florida lottery. What an amazing waste of money! The week I saw this man make his "investment" at a convenience store, the Florida lottery was up to $80 million. But his investment was completely wiped out and, frankly, his chance of winning in his lifetime is slim to none. Yet if he were to invest that

$100 a week in a solid no-load mutual fund (per my instructions in this book), he would have $5,200 invested the first year and $52,000 in ten years. Assuming a 15 percent annualized return for 15 years, his investment would be worth $295,000! Needless to say, his chances of winning this jackpot are far higher than the Florida lottery.

Last year, I was leaving the Las Vegas Money Show, an investment conference, and a taxi driver told me his story. Thirty years ago, he said, he turned $97 into $300 in his first trip to Vegas. Excited by his winnings, he decided to sell his house, his car, and all his belongings, intent on getting rich by gambling. He returned to Las Vegas with $13,000 in cash—and in one week he was flat broke! Now he was driving a cab. At the airport, I paid the fare, then gave the cab driver a silver dollar and a copy of my newsletter, *Forecasts & Strategies*. "Your luck is about to change," I said. Today, of course, I'd give him a copy of *Thirty-Day Plan to Financial Independence*.

The Earlier You Start, the Better

One more piece of advice: The sooner you begin your regular investment program, the quicker you'll reach financial success.

The following example dramatically demonstrates this point. I call it the Bonnie and Clyde story. Bonnie wants to marry Clyde and settle down. Clyde is more interested in robbing banks and playing the casinos and tells Bonnie they'll get married when they have enough money to be set for life.

Bonnie decides to get a job and start a nest egg. She begins investing and puts aside $1,000 a year for the next ten years, averaging a 10 percent a year return. Meantime, Clyde continues to spend everything he steals. Finally, after ten years, Bonnie shows Clyde her investment statement, now worth $17,531 ($10,000 original investment plus $7,531 in profits earned over ten years). Clyde, impressed by Bonnie's return and concerned about setting an example, learns the error of his ways and decides to go legit.

They get married and Bonnie quits her job to raise a family. Imitating Bonnie's investment program, he invests $1,000 a year for the rest of his life.

Even though Bonnie quits her job and cannot add any more to her account, she continues to earn a 10 percent a year return on her principal. No new funds are invested. Meanwhile, Clyde continues to add $1,000 a year for the remainder of his life.

Here's the question: Which investment account does better over the next thirty years? Bonnie, who invests only a total of $10,000? Or Clyde, who starts investing ten years later and keeps investing for the rest of his life?

The results are surprising. Bonnie stops investing additional funds into her account after ten years, yet her account stays ahead of Clyde's account, even though Clyde is adding to his account every year. In fact, Clyde is falling farther and farther behind Bonnie. The difference in the accounts is $17,531 after ten years, $29,934 after twenty years, and $54,937 after thirty years. Clyde can never catch up with Bonnie, unless he adds more than $1,000 to his account each year, or somehow earns more than 10 percent.

The lesson? It pays to invest early! The sooner you start your AIP, the better off you will be.

Two Principles You Must Never Forget

As a financial counselor, I often hear this question, "Mr. Skousen, what's the secret to becoming independently wealthy?"

The answer is not necessarily to earn more income. If you are a spendthrift, earning more income won't inevitably solve your financial problems. After all, millionaires have become bankrupt because they never learned how to control their spending. Wayne Newton, a Las Vegas entertainer, is a perfect example. He filed for bankruptcy even though he made millions each year. He blamed his advisors who got him into leveraged real estate ventures, but

BONNIE VS. CLYDE

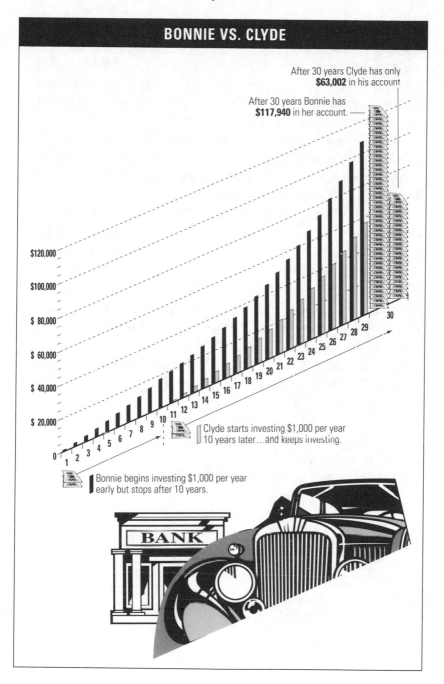

After 30 years Clyde has only **$63,002** in his account

After 30 years Bonnie has **$117,940** in her account. —

$120,000

$100,000

$ 80,000

$ 60,000

$ 40,000

$ 20,000

0

1 2 3 4 5 6 7 8 9 10 11 12 13 14 15 16 17 18 19 20 21 22 23 24 25 26 27 28 29 30

Clyde starts investing $1,000 per year 10 years later…and keeps investing.

Bonnie begins investing $1,000 per year early but stops after 10 years.

BANK

ultimately he personally is responsible for not living within his means.

The real key to financial success can be found in two simple principles. First, develop a consistent, regular savings program. If you save regularly, it means that you are always spending less than your income, and thus building wealth.

It's important to note in this regard that saving money regularly does not mean you have to live a stingy lifestyle. In fact, as long as you are saving regularly, you can spend as much as you want, whatever your net income permits.

This reminds me of the story of Arkad, the fabled character who became the richest man in Babylon. As George Clason relates in *The Richest Man in Babylon*, "In old Babylon there once lived a certain very rich man named Arkad. Far and wide he was famed for his wealth. Also he was famed for liberality. He was generous in his charities. He was generous with his family. He was liberal in his own expenses. But nevertheless each year his wealth increased more rapidly than he spent it."

By the way, *The Richest Man in Babylon* is a book I strongly recommend for your financial library (see Day 28). It will change your life!

Of course, Arkad started out very poor as a chariot maker but, by following the two principles outlined here, he became the richest man in Babylon.

To find out the second principle of financial success, read my advice for Day 4.

ACTIONS TO TAKE ON DAY 3

1. Decide how much you want to invest out of every paycheck.

2. Be realistic, but pick a number that you think you can afford (such as 10 percent).

3. Remember: budgets don't usually work. Arrange to have the money automatically withheld from your paycheck or bank account.

4. If you have not started an automatic wealth building account, do it now. It pays to start early.

DISCOVER THE RIGHT
INVESTMENT FOR YOU

Yesterday, we learned the first principle of financial success: Save on a regular basis.

The second principle is to put your savings to good use. Saving regularly will put you on the road to success, but it is the productive use of savings that helps you reach your destination. My doctor friend put his savings in a money market fund. That was a good investment in the early 1980s, when yields exceeded 16 percent, but today, with rates as low as 4-5 percent, you're not likely to get rich.

Remember, nobody ever got rich on a passbook savings account, except the banks. No one got rich investing in treasury bills, except the government.

To make investing exciting, you need to make more than 4-5 percent. In fact, investing only becomes exciting when you can move into double-digit returns, so you can double or triple your money in a few short years. When you make big profits fast, it stimulates your desire to save and earn more. Profits beget profits!

Invest productively, and you'll be super-successful. How do you invest productively? There are two basic ways: Invest in your own successful business or invest in other people's successful businesses. In other words, invest in free enterprise. You'll make mistakes, but you'll learn from your mistakes and eventually make big money. Most of the people on the Forbes list of 400 Richest People in America made it by operating their own businesses. On Day 17 we'll discuss the important points about starting your own business and the best ways to go about it.

For now, if you aren't inclined to start your own business, the next best thing you can do is invest in other people's successful businesses—that is, invest in the stock market! Contrary to popular opinion, stocks are not lottery tickets, but part ownership in ongoing businesses. And many of them are growing and earning money consistently. In his excellent book, *How to Be Rich*, J. Paul Getty says the best way to become wealthy is to invest in businesses that are "bound to burgeon over time." (You'll be adding Getty's book to your financial success library—see Day 28.)

Automatic Wealth Builder Shows You the Way

The Automatic Wealth Builder, introduced on Day 2, shows you how to maximize your profits in the stock market. Schwab offers over two hundred no-load mutual funds that invest in stocks, bonds, and other investments. ("No load" means that you pay no commission when you buy or sell. All your money goes to work for you immediately.) These are managed by some of the top money managers in the world.

The Automatic Wealth Builder incorporates the two basic

principles of financial success: first, saving regularly, and second, investing profitably. Here are the advantages of this investment account:

- ◆ growth potential of 10-50 percent per year
- ◆ high likelihood that your account will increase in value from year to year (because of diversification and because you are adding to it every month)
- ◆ one simple form to set up
- ◆ maintenance by one of the largest brokerage houses in the world
- ◆ no time or effort required to monitor investments
- ◆ consolidated monthly statements at no charge
- ◆ minimum initial investment, usually only $1,000, and sometimes less
- ◆ availability to anyone of any income level or age, working or retired
- ◆ ideal investment plan for future business, home buying, retirement, child's education, or spending money
- ◆ value traceable every business day
- ◆ automatic diversification
- ◆ broad choice of investment alternatives from over two hundred mutual funds
- ◆ professional, top-rated fund managers
- ◆ no commissions or loads to invest
- ◆ buy, sell, or trade among funds at no commission
- ◆ no trading required
- ◆ no pushy broker (in fact, the broker never calls you)
- ◆ no penalties for early withdrawal

♦ tax advantages—qualifies for long-term capital gains treatment if you hold funds for more than a year

♦ sell at any time without commissions

♦ investment choices monitored monthly in my newsletter, *Forecasts & Strategies* (800-777-5005)

The account I'm describing is the Automatic Investment Plan (AIP), as developed by Schwab, Fidelity, and Jack White. As you can see, I'm extremely impressed with AIP, so much so that I've opened accounts for myself and my family. So far the account has never lost money.

AIP is simple. First, you open an account at Schwab (or other discount brokerage firm). Then you fill out the one-page AIP form. You decide how much money you want withheld from your paycheck or checking account. You can invest automatically every two weeks, monthly, or quarterly, depending on your desires and your ability to meet the minimum investment requirement. After you meet the minimum investment for the fund(s) you select, you can invest as little as $250 per period (semimonthly, monthly, or quarterly). If you can't make the minimum investment or minimum periodic payments, see the advice of Day 5 on how to raise cash to meet the investment minimums.

After you establish your AIP, your investment program runs automatically. No more time spent worrying about your investment portfolio or having to remember to save. It's all done for you at no charge.

How Does Schwab Do It?

You may be wondering, how can Schwab (and other brokerage houses) offer no-load mutual funds without commissions? Obviously, they aren't in the charity business. The answer is that Schwab makes money by making a financial arrangement with each fund family. Basically, each fund rebates to Schwab a portion of its annual administrative fee, typically between 0.25 percent and 0.35 percent annually. Most funds charge shareholders 1-2 percent in annual administrative fees, so they can afford to give up a small percentage to Schwab, especially when new business is coming in by the millions each year through Schwab's no-commission program. Moreover, participation in the Schwab program reduces some of the fund's expenses because the fund families don't have to spend as much on outside advertising. Clearly, it's a win-win deal for Schwab and the funds, and therefore I expect to see many more funds signing up with Schwab in the future.

The Best Investments: My Top Recommendations

I recommend that you consider two approaches when you start your Automatic Wealth Builder with Schwab & Co.

The first method is what I call the Harry Browne approach. Renowned financial expert Harry Browne has developed what he calls a "permanent" portfolio of four investment categories:

- ◆ 25 percent stocks
- ◆ 25 percent bonds
- ◆ 25 percent gold
- ◆ 25 percent cash

Browne has demonstrated that a permanent portfolio divided equally among these four categories will give you a well-diversified investment plan that will protect you in almost any condition—inflation or deflation, prosperity or depression, bull or bear market.

If inflation takes off, stocks and bonds may falter, but gold will rise sharply—it is hoped enough to offset the losses in stocks and bonds. If a deflationary depression hits, quality bonds will rise in value and cash will hold steady, but stocks and gold may decline in value. If the world enjoys noninflationary prosperity, stocks should perform the best, while gold will probably languish. There should be, and are, very few periods when the permanent portfolio declines in value.

The declines, moreover, are virtually eliminated if you adjust the portfolio at the beginning of each year so that each category is equally represented by 25 percent of the portfolio. For example, if gold doubles in value during the year, then next year, you would sell gold until it once again represented only 25 percent of the entire portfolio.

Add to the permanent portfolio as you would to an AIP—by adding a sum of money to your account each month—and you can see that this permanent portfolio becomes an investment account that never stops growing!

If you are adding to your account automatically each month, the likelihood that your account will be worth less a year later is relatively small. For example, if you have $100,000 in your account and you're adding $1,000 a month, your underlying funds would have to lose more than 12 percent during the year for your account to show a decline. As Browne has demonstrated, that's unlikely in a permanent portfolio fashioned as above.

A no-load mutual fund that applies the Harry Browne philosophy is available. It's called the Permanent Portfolio Fund. Managed by Terry Coxon, the fund has been in existence since 1982, with an annualized return of 4.5 percent. Recently, it has provided double-digit returns. The Permanent Portfolio Fund can be purchased through Schwab, but unfortunately it is not, at this writing, part of Schwab's AIP. If it joins the Schwab program, it might be a well-diversified investment vehicle for those who would like to invest automatically and permanently without worry about the future.

Given that the Permanent Portfolio Fund is not yet part of the Schwab AIP, how can you create your own permanent portfolio? Here are four alternative funds, each representing one of the investment categories, with a heavy emphasis on global investing. Note that each is available in Schwab's AIP.

A SAMPLE PERMANENT PORTFOLIO		
	Recommended Fund	**Minimum Initial Investment**
25% stocks	Janus Worldwide Fund	$1,000/$250
25% bonds	Warburg-Pincus Global Fixed Income Fund	$ 250/$250
25% gold	United Services World Gold	$1,000/$250
25% cash	Schwab Money Market Fund	$1,000/$250

Once you've established this permanent portfolio, you can contribute as little as $250 per month or per quarter to keep your investment growing.

For Those Who Want Totally Tax-Free Income

By the way, Schwab's plan offers an excellent opportunity for those who want to live off tax-free income entirely. Simply invest monthly or quarterly in one or more tax-free municipal bond funds. Recommended tax-free funds are Dreyfus General Municipal Bond Fund, Strong Municipal Bond Fund, Stein Rowe High-Yield Municipals. Then sit back and collect your tax-free income.

An Aggressive Growth Portfolio

If you wish to take a little more risk, you might be able to improve upon your long-term performance by choosing my second alternative, Warburg-Pincus Global. Schwab has already signed up over two hundred funds to participate in this service, so there's plenty to choose from. Some of the major fund families, such as Scudder, T. Rowe Price, Vanguard, and Fidelity, have not joined the Schwab program yet, but there are plenty of good funds to choose from already.

I monitor the best funds in each issue of my newsletter, *Forecasts & Strategies*. At the present time, here are my favorites in each category:

GROWTH PORTFOLIO		
	Recommended Fund	**Minimum Initial Investment**
International Stocks	20th Centu:, Int. Equity	$ 250
Emerging Markets	Lexington Worldwide E. M.	$1,000
U.S. Stocks	20th Century Ultra	$ 250
Communications	Montgomery Global Comm.	$2,000
Quality U.S. Bonds	Dreyfus A Bonds Plus	$1,000
High-Yield Bonds	Federated High Yield Trust	$ 250
Tax-free Munis.	Dreyfus Gen. Muni. Bond	$1,000
Int'l Bonds	Warburg-Pincus Global Fixed Income	$ 250
Energy	Rushmore American Gas Ind	$1,000
Gold	United Services World Gold	$1,000
Utilities	INVESCO Strategic Utilities	$ 250

If I were to choose from the above funds for maximum profitability and diversification over the long term, I would opt for the following five funds:

♦   20th Century International Equity

♦   Lexington Worldwide Emerging Markets

♦   20th Century Ultra

♦   Montgomery Global Communications

♦   United Services World Gold

These five funds offer tremendous profit potential, global diversification, and hedging. They are the funds for the nineties. In fact, they are the five funds I am personally investing in on a monthly basis.

I will monitor these five investment funds on a regular basis in *Forecasts & Strategies* and many of the other funds listed above as well. I recommend most of these funds for long-term appreciation, but if there is a change, I'll alert you in my monthly report. You never know when a better fund will come along.

ACTIONS TO TAKE ON DAY 4

1. Choose investments in your AIP that will preserve your capital and increase in value over the long run.
2. Decide whether you are a conservative or aggressive investor, and select your investment choices among those described in this chapter.

DAY 5

RAISE INSTANT CASH AT HOME

What if you don't have the funds to meet the minimum investment requirements for specific funds (typically $1,000 to $5,000 for each fund)?

How can you raise additional cash to add to your Schwab investment account, to make your money work for you and grow faster? You'd be amazed how many assets you have that are just sitting there wasting away when they could be put to work making money for you!

Here are ways to raise the money this month.

A Garage (Estate) Sale

You'd be surprised how much "cash" is lying around. All you have to do is sell these unused or unneeded assets. How much can you raise from well-planned garage sales? Try upwards of $500— for a weekend!

Garage sales are magnets for money. People from all walks of life like to get a bargain. I've seen millionaires and hobos show up at sales. The millionaires are in search of some precious artwork that may have gotten shoved behind a worthless painting or simply to take advantage of the ignorance of the seller. Regardless of their motives, they are out there, just waiting to buy something.

Most people who show up at the sales are in search of knick-knacks that appeal to them. Don't underestimate the tastes of others. The saying "one person's trash is another person's treasure" holds more water at garage sales than just about anywhere else.

You can have a garage sale once a month and make $500 or more to add to your savings. Obviously, you are thinking that you don't have enough junk in your house to sell every month to make that kind of money. You're right! The way to make this low-profile weekend jaunt into a high-powered income generator is to make a business out of it. When you run out of items to sell or your inventory is dwindling, go to other garage sales and buy from them. The same principle applies—you are looking for a bargain, except this time you are in the market to resell.

One word of advice before you get going on this project: Don't call your sale a garage sale. Call it an estate sale. After all, you are selling items that belong to your estate. An advertised estate sale will attract more of the "big money" people who are in search of old treasures.

Advertise your garage or estate sale in the local newspaper. Most newspapers have a section in the classifieds on Thursday, Friday, and Saturday, that offer free or low-cost ads for garage sales. In your ad, make sure you include specific times for the sale and add the phrase "no early birds" or you'll have people waking you up at 5 a.m. to look at your wares. Also, be sure that every

item is clearly marked with a price—this allows you time to bargain instead of quoting prices every two seconds.

You must be willing to bargain at a garage sale. Rarely will anyone pay you full price for an item. Remember, people are looking
for bargains—if they want to pay full price, they will go to a
department store. Mark your prices up about 30 percent higher
than your bottom-line price. If you are not sure of the price you
should charge, go to several nearby garage sales and check
prices—but don't buy! One exception: If you see an incredible
"steal," you may want to buy the item... and sell it at a higher
price. Recent example: An astute shopper picked up a Park Astec
pen for only $55 at a garage sale, then sold it to a specialty dealer
for $15,000! These occurrences don't happen often, but when
they do, it's a thrill of a lifetime.

Most people will offer you between 20 percent and 40 percent
under the marked price. You can settle somewhere in between.
Don't be too anxious to sell—you want customers to feel they
have found a bargain and worked hard to get it. That's part of the
fun at these sales.

If you are not inclined to have a garage sale at your home, for whatever reason, you can usually rent a booth at your local flea market to
sell your wares. It might cost you $10 or $15 per day for the booth,
but you will also have thousands more people to sell to. Or you can
participate in a neighborhood sale, located at someone else's house.

Collecting Unpaid Debts

At some time or another you may have lent money or sold
something to a friend or relative and never been paid. Because of
the close relationship, you have been reluctant to apply any pressure on the borrower or buyer to pay up. This weakness has cost
people hundreds of dollars. It may be a communication problem
more than anything else. But instead of feeling embarrassed to ask
for money that is rightfully yours, you should feel upset that the
payment is so long overdue. Imagine if your bank were mistaken-

ly to withdraw more money than was due from your account for a direct payment on a loan. Would you just sit around and wait for them to find the error and reimburse your account? Chances are you would rush down to the bank and read them the riot act.

Yet when someone you know is holding out on you, you are often willing to let it go indefinitely. Make a resolution to contact each person who owes you money and begin to collect. Chances are they have legitimately forgotten about the debt and are more than happy to pay you. You will never know unless you ask.

Moreover, they may feel guilty about how long overdue the payment is, and will actually be relieved to discuss it and set up a repayment plan. Before you talk to them, practice what you will say. Focus on the debt, not the person. Above all, remain calm and resolute.

Big Ticket Items

Big ticket items such as jewelry or electronics can produce much higher returns through a private sale than a garage sale. Although the garage sale is an avenue for disposal, most shoppers are out for low-priced bargains. Pawn shops will pay you less than half what the item is worth, if that. Your best source for a high-dollar sale is the classified section of your newspaper. The ad may cost you a few dollars, but you can increase your return significantly.

Classifieds

Classified ads are read for the most part by serious buyers. These folks are looking for a specific item and have the cash in hand to buy it. It is a sale waiting to happen. Always place your ads so they appear in the Friday and weekend editions of the paper. The Friday and Sunday editions are the two most widely circulated issues.

These are just a few examples of how you can raise money quickly from assets that you are not using or just don't need anymore. Unfortunately, many people are pack-rats, refusing to part with anything. This situation usually results in a huge collection of deterioriating or unusable merchandise that will eventually find its way to the dumpster. Don't be one of these people. Instead, make your assets contribute to a better quality of life for you and your family.

Don't Worry about Taxes

One more piece of advice: Don't worry about paying taxes on items you sell at your "estate" sale. You don't owe taxes on items that you sell for less than what you paid for them. Of course, if you make a business of buying low at other garage sales and then selling those items at a higher price at yours, you will owe tax on the difference.

ACTIONS TO TAKE ON DAY 5

1. That stuff in your basement or garage isn't junk, it's assets! Sell it for cash.

2. Go through your garage, basement, and other areas of your house, and ask yourself, "Wouldn't I rather have cash to invest?" Make a list of potential sales items.

3. Set a day to have an "estate" sale, and place an ad in the weekend edition of your newspaper.

4. Today, place a classified ad to sell one big ticket item you no longer use.

5. List all the people who owe you money and drop them a note reminding them you want it back. Arrange a follow-up meeting.

GET READY, GET SET, GO!
Fill out the Forms and Send Them In

Today you are on your way! You should have received the account opening forms from Charles Schwab or another discount broker by now. Today you will fill out these forms and send them in. On this day we will go over step by step what you need to do to fill out the Schwab application for (1) opening an account and (2) the Automatic Investment Plan (AIP). We'll go over everything one step at a time, considering all the options.

Opening Your Investment Account

The Schwab Account Application is easy to fill out. Part 1 asks for a lot of personal information, including name, address, telephone number, and employment. Some information is required (Social Security number), other information is not (driver's license number, occupation).

The application includes room for a joint account. Generally, I recommend a joint account if you are married. It will save trouble if one of you dies unexpectedly.

Part 2, "Financial Profile," is now required by the securities association. But you do not need to list your exact income or net worth. Choose among several broad categories. Unless you are planning to trade options, futures, or on margin, the level of your income and net worth is not important to the broker. (If you don't know what options, futures, and on margin are, you shouldn't get involved with them.)

Part 3, "Account Handling Instructions," informs you that Schwab will automatically hold all your stock and bond certificates for you. If you want to take personal possession of these certificates, you need to inform Schwab.

Part 4 asks you to choose a money market fund for parking your daily cash. Choose among six funds. If you live in New York and want to avoid state income taxes, pick the New York Municipal Cash Trust Shares. If you live in California and want to avoid state income taxes, choose Schwab California Tax-Exempt Money Fund. If you want to avoid federal income taxes on your dividends, choose Schwab Tax-Exempt Money Fund. If you want maximum dividend return, choose Schwab Money Market Fund.

Part 5 is about your form of payment. You can open an account by sending in a personal check or securities ($1,000 minimum) or by transferring funds from another brokerage account (Schwab will provide a transfer form for this).

Part 6 asks you to sign the form and date it.

Part 7 asks if you wish to buy securities on margin. Margin allows you to purchase stocks and bonds with borrowed funds. I don't recommend it for new investors. If you don't want to buy securities on margin, don't sign the form.

That's all there is to it. After you've filled out the form and signed it, place the form in a Schwab envelope along with your check and mail it. You'll receive confirmation in a few weeks.

Schwab One Account

You can also opt for a Schwab One Account, which offers additional benefits, including a checkbook for easy withdrawal of your cash and a VISA debit card. A VISA debit card acts like a VISA credit card, except that funds are withdrawn immediately from your Schwab account to pay for any expenditures by using your VISA card.

The form is similar to the regular Schwab Account Application. The major difference is the minimum—$5,000 for a Schwab One account rather than $1,000 for the regular account.

I believe the Schwab One Account is worth having if you meet the minimum. But it is not a necessary step in achieving financial independence under our system.

Automatic Investment Plan

The second form you need to fill out on Day 6 is the Schwab AIP form.

Part A asks for "General Information": Check the box, "New Automatic Investment Plan." List your name and joint account name (if applicable) and your address. Under "Start Date," list next month and the year. Give your Social Security number. List your Schwab Account number. If you don't have it yet, leave it blank. It can be assigned by Schwab when they receive your account open form. Check which account type you have— brokerage, Schwab One, or Individual Retirement Account.

How Much Should You Invest Regularly?

At this stage, you need to decide how much to invest on a regular, automatic basis. The amount you choose is entirely up to you, as long as you meet the minimum, which is typically $250 per time period (twice monthly, monthly, or quarterly).

Try to keep it simple. Let me suggest a very simple approach—the "10 Percent Solution." Figure how much your take-home pay is and have 10 percent invested automatically in your investment account. It's easy to figure, and when you get a raise or earn more money, you can easily determine 10 percent each time and increase your monthly or quarterly contributions.

Suppose you take home $2,000 a month. Ten percent is $200, less than the minimum investment amount. Since this does not meet the minimum monthly requirement, you will either have to increase the monthly contribution to $250, or invest $600 quarterly. Either way is fine.

Choosing the Right Funds

Part B requires you to select one or more mutual funds to invest in on a regular basis. You must choose from among the several hundred mutual funds listed with Schwab's One Source. An updated list is contained in your packet. We already discussed my favorite funds on Day 4. Go back and review which funds you like, or choose one of your own, based on your own research. (It might be a good idea to check with *Morningstar* or *Value Line*, two services that rank the track records of mutual funds, before making your decision. You can obtain current issues at your local library.)

When you've made the choice, list the name of the fund(s), their symbols (listed in the brochure accompanying the packet), and the amount you wish to invest on a regular basis.

Part C, "Suitability," requests information about your investment objectives, annual income, net worth, and federal income tax bracket. Be as general as possible.

Sign the form, date it, and return it in Schwab's envelope.

You're all finished. Now sit back, relax, and enjoy becoming wealthy the easy way.

ACTIONS TO TAKE ON DAY 6

1. Fill out the account opening form for Schwab or other discount broker.
2. Fill out the AIP form, identifying which funds you wish to invest in.
3. Mail both forms today.
4. Congratulations! You're on your way to financial independence.

REVIEW AND MEDITATION

Today is a day of rest and contemplation. It is a day to review what you have achieved so far.

The idea of taking off a day for rest and prayerful meditation is very much a part of the Judeo-Christian code. Jews and Christians rest every seventh day, Jews on Saturday and most Christians on Sunday.

The idea of a seventh day of rest fits perfectly with the system we have developed in *Thirty-Day Plan to Financial Independence.* Cultures have learned over the generations that society functions best when its members develop patterns of behavior. Religions require their members to meet once a week to renew their spirits and their friendships. Clubs meet once a week or once a month. If church members met only when they felt like it, how long would the church last? Or the club?

Like most Americans, I have an exercise routine. On Mondays, Wednesdays, and Fridays at noon, I play basketball for an hour. On Tuesdays, Thursdays, and Saturdays, I lift weights, run, and go swimming. On Sundays, I rest. If I didn't have a routine, what shape would I be in?

We all have patterns and routines to maintain our lifestyles and attitudes. The dentist's office reminds you twice a year to have a cleaning and a checkup. The doctor's office calls you for your annual physical. The media remind all of us to pay our taxes on April 15. I'm sure you can think of many other examples.

Shouldn't you also have a financial routine? The Automatic Wealth Builder develops a powerful pattern of wealth building, and it works extremely well.

We All Need Crutches

The longer I live, the more I realize that everyone needs a crutch to help support himself in some way—whether in business, home life, or play. For example, to improve family life, it's a good idea to gather the family together regularly to discuss common problems, goals, or just to enjoy one another. My wife and I tried to gather the family together whenever we remembered, but things always came up and we seldom met. Finally, we decided to set aside Sunday evening for our family meeting, and it has worked ever since. Everyone in our family knows not to plan anything else on that night.

Tricks That Make Your Life Easier

Lots of other supports are being developed to simplify and improve our lives. Several years ago Harry Lorayne in *The Memory Book* revealed some simple, yet powerful, techniques to improve your memory, using the "link," "peg," and "substitute word" methods. It really works. One guy used his method to memorize the symbols of every stock listed on the New York Stock Exchange.

Recently I came across a fantastic new method of learning foreign languages, developed by Professor Dan Mikels. His system relies on basic strategies that do not require conjugating verbs—the most difficult part of learning any language. I'm using his system to learn Spanish, French, and German, and it's amazingly effective.

Make It Simple

In many ways, Schwab's Automatic Investment Plan is an exciting new breakthrough in simplifying your financial life and making it easier to achieve your goals in life. Think of it as a reservoir, where a small stream is flowing into a body that is ever-enlarging in size. You will be surprised at how fast this reservoir grows. Just as a small leak will sink a great ship, so a small stream will fill a huge body to overflowing in no time at all.

This reminds me of something I did recently. Our swimming pool was getting low, so one night I put the hose in the pool and started filling it. It filled up so slowly that I didn't notice it and I forgot that I had left the water on. The next morning the pool was overflowing.

Imagine that happening to your investments. At first it seems like a trickle. But your investment program is so automatic that you forget about it, and one day you suddenly discover that it's overflowing in surplus income!

The average person will have over a million dollars pass through his hands during his lifetime. How much of that money will you hold onto? For most Americans, not enough. But for you, it will be different. You have in your hands the magic formula to catch a steady stream of all the money that is flowing through your hands.

What Do You Want to Do with All That Money?

Day 7 is a good time to reflect on what you want to do with all the money that you will be building over the next few years.

Your independent investment account can provide money for

♦ your children's education

♦ a new house

♦ seed capital for a new business

♦ emergencies and other short-term demands

♦ supplemental retirement income

♦ venture capital (loans) to other people's promising businesses

♦ a charitable cause

♦ travel and vacations

Today is a good time to think specifically about what you plan to do with your independent investment funds. By dreaming about using your money, you will be more likely to continue the program. Take a few moments and contemplate your dreams.

Make It a Fun Game

One final thought. Nothing is more satisfying than receiving in the mail each month a statement from Charles Schwab & Co., your Investment Account That Never Stops Growing! I get excited every time I receive it, anticipating how much my account is going to be worth this month.

Oh, by the way, I just got my latest statement. The value of my account is up to $30,000. Nice feeling.

When you see how much your account has grown in the past month, quarter, and year, you want to see it grow more. Success breeds success! You want to add to your account, make it grow even faster. You will start reading the business page of the newspaper, not just the sports or style section. You have a goal in mind—financial independence—and the faster you can succeed, the better. So you may find yourself adding to your account from time to time. When you get a raise at work or make more profits in your business, you may wish to increase the monthly contribution. I recently raised my monthly contribution from $1,000 a month to $1,250. It's something that grows on you.

Why Your Account Can't Help but Grow and Grow and Grow...

Yesterday, on Day 6, I recommended that you set aside 10 percent of your take-home pay for your monthly investment plan. Ten percent is easy to figure when you first get started, and it also makes it easy to keep your investment amount current. Each time you get a raise or a bonus, simply increase your savings so it still represents 10 percent. It's that simple.

Note that you aren't putting all your increased income into your investment plan, just 10 percent. You have 90 percent for spending money.

In essence, you have three things going for you that will tend to increase the value of your investment account each year: first, your automatic contributions will add funds to your account each month; second, you will tend to increase your monthly contributions whenever you get a raise or an increase in income (based on the 10 percent principle); and third, your mutual funds will tend to increase over time as the underlying investments (stocks and bonds) gain in price and dividends are automatically reinvested.

Good luck and welcome aboard!

ACTIONS TO TAKE ON DAY 7

1. Set aside the seventh day for leisure and contemplation.
2. Establish a financial routine.
3. Dream about how to spend your money.
4. Go find something to enjoy doing with your family that doesn't require spending money.
5. Thank God for your good fortune, good health, and good friends.

SECOND WEEK:
Reduce Your
Expenses Immediately

HAVE A FINANCIAL CHECKUP!
Income and Expenses

Here's a new way of looking at your financial situation.

Consider your personal finances as you would a publicly trad-ed company with shareholders represented by your family. In order to produce the most gains for your shareholders, you have to run an efficient, growing organization. In order to appease the outside auditors, creditors, and the like, you have to make sure your books are squeaky clean today—and that they will remain so in the future. Public companies are always being analyzed, both by internal accountants and by independent analysts. This is what keeps them on their toes, finding ways to make more money and to squeeze more out of each dollar. The companies that fail this test usually wind up as the market's losers. If they are effective, their stock prices go up. This principle is true of your family "corporation" as well.

A Step-by-Step Approach

The first step is to initiate an internal audit. We will be discussing your assets and liabilities in Financial Checkup II, on Day 22. For today, just analyze your income and expenses, since these determine whether your personal holding company (your family) will end each day in the black or in the red. Ultimately, it is how much you earn and spend each day that will determine your total assets and liabilities in the future.

The Income Side

Begin with this month's records. Determining your income should be fairly easy, since we tend to get paid less frequently than we pay others, and we have to keep records for tax purposes. Include all your income—salary, refund checks, commissions, gifts, and, since this is a family corporation, your children's incomes, too. Your children may balk at this, insisting that what they earn is "their" money, to use as they please. Such an attitude leads to skewed expectations in the future, however, as teens who grow accustomed to spending all their money on discretionary consumption suddenly discover the realities of day-to-day living as adults. Better to let them be a part of your budgeting process, even though you don't charge them room and board, so they quickly learn the realities of home repairs, insurance costs, carrying charges, and the importance of saving.

Be sure to include all sources of income and all expenditures. Here is a brief list of sources that you might overlook:

♦ take-home pay from your job or business—this should include all income from sources that would issue you a W-2 form or a 1099

♦ commissions

♦ pension/Social Security/disability income—can include benefits from retirement income, injury, and/or disability

♦ alimony or child support

♦ dividend/investment income—includes income from stocks, bonds, real estate, loans, certificates of deposit, interest from checking and savings accounts

♦ trust fund proceeds

♦ miscellaneous income from temporary business ventures such as garage sales or sales of assets

In certain cases income will not be realized until later in the year—quarterly dividend payments, for example, or year-end bonuses. In this case, estimate how much you expect to make. But be realistic. Don't fall into the trap of assuming you will have a great sales year, just so you can justify a major expenditure. If your business is seasonal or linked to commission sales, then it is better to use a historical estimate of your income, assuming a low average rather than high, just to be safe. An average of the past three years income should allow you to make a reasonable estimate, taking into account the cyclical nature of most businesses.

The Expenditure Side

Next, categorize and total your monthly expenditures. Start with your check stubs and credit card statements. Try to be as specific as possible—don't just write "Mastercard, $500," but "Dinner at Chi-Chi's, $xx; athletic shoes for Junior, $xx; dental checkups, $xx." And be sure to include the interest paid on credit cards and installment loans as a separate category. (Incidentally, if you are charging medical and dental bills on your credit card, you are wasting money each month! Work out a payment schedule with your doctor, and stop paying double-digit interest rates.) Include in your list money that has been set aside for taxes, investments, and any payments that are automatically deducted from your checking account. I have included a sample chart at the end of this chapter for you to use in getting started.

As you total the items recorded in your checkbook and credit card statements, you will probably discover that your expenditure list is much smaller than your income list, indicating a nice surplus for savings. Right?

Unfortunately, no. True, your estimated expenditures list will probably be small, but that money is not likely to be in your mattress or cookie jar. It has been spent, as cash, and you have no record of your true spending patterns. It's time now to wrack your collective brains and try to remember where the cash has gone. How much do you usually cash for day-to-day expenses each week, and how is it distributed? Allowances and lunch money? Gas for the cars? Fast food or groceries? Try to draw as accurate a picture of your family's spending patterns as you can.

Now compare income and expenditures again. If the difference is only 10 percent to 15 percent of your total income, go ahead and move on to the next step, knowing that you have a reasonably accurate picture of your spending history. I will show you how to be more precise in the future. However, if you still have no idea where your money has been going (and most Americans don't!), it is time to start what I call the "No-Budget Budget." *Begin today to write down everything you spend, no matter how small.* Insist that family members do this as well. Keep track of your expenditures for thirty days, and then return to this chapter for the rest of Financial Checkup I.

Step 2 requires you to make a similar assessment of your income and expenditures for previous months, going back as far as you can, preferably for a full year. This allows you to adjust for seasonal changes in your income and expenditures, and gives you a clearer picture of your financial foibles. It also allows you to average in the cost of expenditures that occur only once or twice a year, such as college tuition or property taxes.

Now you can see a complete picture of your spending patterns, and begin creating a budget tailor-made for your family. As you review your history, you will be appalled at some of your spending habits and proud of others. Most important, by seeing the total amount you have spent for items in certain categories, and contrasting that with other items offering greater satisfaction that you might have purchased if you had been more aware of your expenditures, you will begin automatically to become a wiser, more satisfied consumer. Tomorrow we will begin examining more specific ways to organize your personal or family budget. This exercise is particularly eye-opening for children, who often think the family purse is bottomless until they begin making spending comparisons. They may even start turning off the bathroom light!

I can't emphasize enough the importance of maintaining the proper balance between income and expenditures. As you dig deeper into you financial history, look for patterns that may signal self-destructing behavior. For example, you would expect that most people experience a healthier financial picture after they receive a raise in income. But for many people, financial security actually worsens when income increases. How is that possible? Because, for many families, when income increases by 10 percent, expenses increase by 20 percent or more, driven by renewed expectations. Purchases that had been delayed, such as replacing the washing machine, repairing the car's air conditioning, updating Mom's wardrobe, or taking a family vacation, all seem possible when the raise comes in. Thanks to the excessive availability of credit cards, it is possible to spend an entire year's raise in the first month.

To avoid falling into this common trap, heed this simple suggestion: When you receive a raise, don't spend any of it for at least six months. Don't even tell anyone about the raise, if you can avoid it! Then add the difference to your savings. Only by increasing your savings will your wealth increase with your income.

Let's get started.

Each individual or family's financial checkup will be different from the rest. The purpose of this review is not to have you conform to any one national standard of living, but simply to chart your own standard of living, to get a picture of your personal financial health as it stands today. Use your checkbook register, credit card statements, receipts, and the following chart to help you identify where your money currently comes from and where it is going. Begin by examining your records for just one month. Then we will be ready to proceed to Day 9, the Financial Freedom, No-Budget Budget.

FINANCIAL CHECK-UP

Item	What you Make / spend	Total %
Income		
Take-home pay (from job or business)	_____	_____
Dividend/interest income (after tax)	_____	_____
Freelance work/home business	_____	_____
Pension/disability/Social Security	_____	_____
Other		
Total Income	_____	100%
Expenses		
Food and beverages	_____	_____
Home consumption	_____	_____
Dining out	_____	_____
Alcoholic beverages	_____	_____
Housing		
Mortgage/rent	_____	_____
Insurance (homeowner/renters)	_____	_____
Property taxes (monthly)	_____	_____

Transportation

    Vehicle (monthly payment)   _____   _____

    Operating maintenance   _____   _____

    Public transportation   _____   _____

    Insurance   _____   _____

Household expenses

    Furniture and appliances   _____   _____

    Utilities   _____   _____

    Telephone/fax   _____   _____

    Lawn care   _____   _____

Other

    Medical care (include health/dental,

      unpaid bills)   _____   _____

    Clothing and jewelry   _____   _____

    Recreation   _____   _____

    Personal business   _____   _____

    Private education (include books, supplies,

      and uniforms)   _____   _____

    Public education (books, supplies)   _____   _____

    Charity   _____   _____

    Personal care   _____   _____

    Tobacco   _____   _____

Total Expenses   _____   _____

Difference between Income and Expenses   _____   100%
(% of income)

If you are spending more than 90 percent of your income, you need to reevaluate your spending habits and sources of income. In the next few days, we'll review the expenditure side of your budget and see how you can cut back without reducing your standard of living.

ACTIONS TO TAKE ON DAY 8

1. Treat your personal finances as you would a publicly traded company.
2. Determine how much you earn and spend each day. Write down *everything* you spend for one month.
3. Use my sample chart.

ADOPT THE FINANCIAL
FREEDOM BUDGET

In order to succeed in restructuring your personal finances, you'll need a tangible game plan. The word "budget" usually elicits a loud groan from most individuals—and with good reason: It seems restrictive, complicated, and ultimately unworkable. If that is true for you, perhaps you are expecting too much from a budget. A budget is simply a tool, not a magic wand, and not a slave driver's whip. It only works as well as the person operating it.

Don't look at a budget as a negative imposition on your lifestyle; after all, your budget is your own creation, not your master. Budgeting can even be fun, especially if you place as much emphasis on the income and savings sides of the equation as you do on the expense side. In a way, it allows you to spend your money twice—

first at the planning stage and then at the actual stage. Often, some simple evaluation at the planning stage will prevent costly mistakes at the actual stage. You've probably never heard of budgeting as being a fun task, but as your financial independence increases, you'll become a wizard at putting every dollar to its best use.

Four-Point Financial Freedom Plan

A well-planned budget is loose enough to allow for the surprises in life, but tight enough to warn you of potential problems before they get out of control. Ideally, for a person with a high level of self-control, a budget should include just four steps:

- automatic savings plan that increases your wealth each time you get paid (Review Day 3)

- short-term savings plan to prepare for seasonal, maintenance, and emergency expenses

- debt avoidance—no credit cards or installment plans

- spending the rest!

Admittedly, this is a plan that must be approached gradually, particularly if you are already living beyond your means. But it is achievable, no matter what your income. It may require some drastic changes in your lifestyle, either on the income side or on the expenditure side, before it can be achieved. But I know several people who have achieved the carefree existence of semiretirement, simply by implementing these four steps. They live within their income, they add to their wealth with each paycheck, and they pay cash for everything. Sometimes their months are fat, and sometimes they are lean, depending on their short-term savings goals. But always they enjoy the serenity of knowing that their financial futures are secure.

Where to Start: The Expenditure Side

We will start with the expenditure side, since that is the place you can see the most immediate and dramatic results. Changing the income side would require some job-hunting or skill development, and you probably don't feel like pounding the pavement today!

Yesterday you made a list of all your income and expenditures. Take that list out now, and analyze the expenditure side more carefully. You will recall numerous items you have purchased that brought you little lasting satisfaction. Why did you buy them? Some wasteful expenditures are made out of habit, others because you haven't taken the time to discover different ways of achieving the same goals, and others because you didn't plan ahead. For example, did you spend $40 taking the family to the movies because everyone wanted to see that particular show or because going to the movies is how you always spend family time on Friday night? Would a picnic at the park have satisfied the same desire for family fun, at less than half the cost? Similarly, did your daughter's tuition really sneak up on you to blow your budget, or did you simply forget to set money aside each month in anticipation of this semiannual expense?

Note also how much of your money is spent on interest payments for various debts: auto, mortgage, credit cards, consolidation loans, and more. Imagine how different your balance sheet might look if all that money could go into short-term savings instead of the black hole of consumer credit. Then resolve firmly to get out of debt and stay there—even if it means making drastic changes to your style of living. You may feel that you have no options, particularly regarding such big-ticket expenditures as rent or mortgage, utilities, transportation, and food. But you can indeed make changes. Consider selling your house and renting a condo, if necessary. Not only would your monthly mortgage payment go down, allowing your savings to increase, but the budget-breaking variables caused by home repair and maintenance would decrease as well. Similarly, the price of taxi service begins to look cheap when compared with the cost of purchasing, servicing, and insuring a teenager's car.

Get the Family Involved

Bring the family together to discuss your discoveries, not in an accusatory manner, but in a spirit of finding ways to work together at becoming financially solvent. Ask each family member to list three items they purchased in the last month that they could have done without, and one item they would like to buy today, if only they hadn't already spent that money. Again, be very encouraging during this exercise, and compliment everyone for his or her contributions. When they announce the items they wish they hadn't purchased, avoid the temptation to say, "That was a stupid thing to buy," or worse, "I told you so."

Playing "Let's Make a Deal" at this family counsel can be an effective demonstration of the compromise necessary in deciding how to allocate finite resources. Begin with enough cash or play money to represent your monthly income. Then, with a great flourish, take away the amount that is normally withheld for taxes. (Tossing this play money into the trash or burning it can help you make your point.) Throw the money used to service your debts into the trash as well. Next, begin sorting the rest of the money into piles marked "Housing," "Food," "Telephone," "Vacation," and so forth.

Let the family participate freely in this allocation game, making deals with one another as they try to distinguish among needs, wants, and wastes. They may be shocked to realize how little discretionary income is left after the fixed bills are paid. Help them to see that when they ask you for money for the latest video game, they may have to give up a new pair of shoes; when one suggests dinner at a restaurant, they may have to give up a month's piano lessons. When the game has run its course (and before it dissolves into bickering), reach into the trash can and pull out the money that was thrown away on debt servicing. Lead your family to conclude that it might be worth the short-term pain of getting out of debt, in order to pay as you go in the future, using the family's entire net income. As your family will quickly discover for itself, being saddled with the consequences of decisions made months or even years earlier drains the family's discretionary income, causing emotional stress and hostility.

Make "we pay as we go" your family motto. Be proud of your self-discipline, and even brag about it occasionally. Living debt free in America is a feat accomplished only by the proud and the few. The self-esteem of being financially solvent is more psychologically satisfying than keeping up with the Joneses—especially when you know that the Joneses are deeply in debt. As a nation, we seem to feel ashamed to say, "I can't afford it." Try saying, "We choose not to afford it" instead.

In order for this extremely loose, four-point financial freedom plan to work, you must have the self-discipline to say no and to recognize the difference between real wants and perceived wants. A "perceived want" is something you didn't know you wanted until you heard about it on television, read about it in the newspaper, or saw it in your neighbor's backyard. In our consumer-driven society, this will not be easy; you may even have to lock up the television for a while. But it will ultimately help you choose only those items you really want and need, rather than filling your house with all the latest junk that you don't need and only thought you wanted.

Perhaps you don't feel ready for the responsibility of such a loosely formed budget, or perhaps you are in such bad shape from overspending that you need the discipline of a formal budget, at least until you get out of debt. There are several budget plans that can work, if you have the motivation to stick with them. I included a sample budget at the end of Day 8, for those who want to use a traditional style budget.

A Quick(en) Solution

If you enjoy working with computers and want more advanced budget devices, one of the most successful tools to track your personal finances is a software program called Quicken.® There are hundreds of home computer packages available, but for less than $30, I have found nothing that matches Quicken's value.

Quicken has all the tools for both personal and professional financial management. And best of all it is the simplest software program I have ever used. I know this sounds like a ringing endorsement for the product—well, it is!

You can use the program to chart your cash flow, investments, assets, liabilities, tax concerns, and bank accounts. The program allows you to set up as many categories for expenses and income as you want. It also provides an instant way to balance your checkbook and also print your checks. Unfortunately it does not print the money to pay the bills....

For more information on Quicken, call 800-624-8742, or look for the software package at any store selling computer supplies.

Budget Nightmares to Avoid

Developing a practical, realistic budget is not an easy task. But by recognizing potential pitfalls in advance, many of them can be avoided, or at least lessened. Expect to make some mistakes, and be prepared with alternative solutions. For example, no matter how meticulous you are in listing the inflows and outflows, there will usually be one or two unexpected or forgotten items. A quarterly or semiannual payment may be overlooked, for example, because it did not show up on a monthly basis in your check register or your bill files. Or the repair that you had planned for the small crack in the swimming pool may turn into a major resurfacing, complete with a crack in an underground pipe.

These may seem like insignificant details on your road to financial independence, but as the famed Russian author Aleksandr Solzhenitsyn once put it, "It's not the sea that drowns you, it's the puddles."

The Family, Again

Another budget faux pas is the lack of family involvement in the development process. Many heads of households take it upon themselves to develop a budget and then present it to the family, usually with a stern lecture that includes a great deal of finger-pointing. This may work in the short term, but for real long-term success the whole family should be involved in the process. This is true for two reasons. First, you need the family. When more individuals are involved, the potential to overlook certain expenses or income sources is diminished. Second, family members may resent your sudden imposition of an austerity plan if they haven't participated in the planning and if they don't understand the benefits such a plan will have for them. Calling the family together for a planning council, or playing the "Let's Make a Deal" game described above, will help you avoid this major pitfall.

Expel the Impulse

The most important risk to anyone's financial health is the tendency to buy without thinking. I developed a proverb to spell out the dangers of such impulse spending: *"One who spends before he thinks, will always spend more than he thinks."*

Here are some suggestions to discuss at your family meeting that will help curb impulsive spending:

◆ Wait a day after you see an item before you return to buy it. If you are worried that the item might be sold before you return, ask that it be held overnight. Chances are that you will decide it just isn't as important to you tomorrow as it seemed to be yesterday, thus avoiding "buyer's regret."

♦ If you like to go to malls or shopping centers to browse and just enjoy the time outside, leave your wallet and checkbook at home. Retailers make it their life's work to find ways to make you part with your money. If you see something that you like, you can always buy it later.

♦ Take your name off catalog mailing lists—you can do this by contacting the catalog distributor and asking that your name be removed from the lists. To have your name removed from most mailing lists, write to Direct Marketing Association, 1120 Avenue of the Americas, New York, New York 10036, 212-768-7277.

♦ Learn to say, "No, thank you." Say no to demonstrations of products, unless you came specifically to shop for that product. Learn to say "just browsing" when you are in a store.

♦ Always consider how much work you put into earning the dollars you are about to spend. This became crystal clear to my son when he stopped for dinner on his way home from his first day at work—and realized that he was eating four hours' worth of labor in just fifteen minutes.

♦ Instead of spending impulsively, why not try impulse saving! Each time you change your mind about buying something, add the money to your investment account. You will be amazed at how much you have at the end of the month, just by avoiding impulse expenditures. If you can master the art of saving money each time you are in the mood for spending, you will be well on your way to financial freedom. A similar trick many people practice is to drop their loose change into a cookie jar each night. Again, you will be surprised at how quickly those dimes and quarters add up. In fact, my wife often takes the children out for ice cream with the pennies she gathers around the house, just to show them how quickly pennies can add up to dollars.

♦ Write everything down! You will tend to think more and consequently spend less.

♦ Finally, be realistic with your no-budget budget. Don't estimate expenditures at an unreasonably low cost, just so the books will balance, and don't overestimate your income, either. If you do, your budget is doomed to fail before it begins. Remember, the reason that most budgets fail is because they are formulated with unreasonable data or objectives and therefore place an emotional as well as financial strain on the family and its ability to function. The purpose of the Financial Freedom budget is to help, not hinder your progress.

The essence of budgeting is to help you become a disciplined spender. Yes, you are allowed to spend money! This book is meant to make your life much better, not more restrictive. The key is discipline. The disciplined spender will automatically live a much healthier financial life than the impulsive spender—that's a given. And that's your goal.

Begin implementing these ideas today. Soon you will be able to pattern your life on the Financial Freedom budget: Save 10 percent automatically; establish short-term savings for nonmonthly expenditures; stay out of debt; spend the rest!

ACTIONS TO TAKE ON DAY 9

1. Adopt the No-Budget budget: Write down all your expenditures.
2. Use my four-step formula, or develop your own.
3. Be realistic—don't underestimate expenditures or overestimate income.
4. Involve your family to maintain accountability in your family budget. Make sure a separate, independent checking account and debit cards are available to your spouse.

DAY

10

EVALUATE YOUR PHYSICAL HEALTH

Ben Franklin said, "Time is money." But the reverse is also true: Money is time! According to recent studies, the higher your income and net worth, the more time you will have—that is, the longer your life expectancy. Most likely, then, if you watch your expenses and build your net worth, you will live longer.

People in higher-income classes tend to live about five to ten years longer than the average person. Recent studies at the University of Michigan show that wealthier individuals enjoy better health, fitness, and quality of life than the average as they age.

It's not just that the rich can buy better medical care. It also has to do with prevention. Wealthier people tend to work in safer occupations, live in lower-crime neighborhoods, and drive safer automobiles. Behavior is also different. Higher-income individuals are usually better educated and as such do not smoke, drink, and overeat as much. They pay closer attention to nutrition and diet. They exercise more. They also tend to live less stressful lives, since they have more financial security. They take more vacations and engage in a greater variety of activities.

Unfortunately many individuals ignore their health while they focus on building their wealth, which results in health problems that may plague them in later years. It is easy to become so overwhelmed by the demands of a growing business that you cut corners in your personal life. My wife and I fell victim to this trap several years ago, when we started our book business. We worked sixteen-hour days, sometimes seven days a week, grabbing fast food on our way to the post office and catnaps while waiting at red lights, until we realized that, unless we made some drastic changes, our children would be very rich and we would be very dead.

Striking a balance between health maintenance and wealth building should not be put off "until you have more time." Plan now to schedule time for rest, exercise, proper nutrition, and regular dental and medical checkups.

Here are my recommendations for living longer, healthier, and more prosperously:

♦ *Increase your net worth steadily and automatically*— By building wealth automatically each month, as outlined in the first week, you will have more financial resources to do the things you want to do, including more time for leisure activities, exercise, and travel. The Automatic Investment Plan increases your financial freedom and security. This long-term wealth building program will also reduce the stress-producing anxiety often associated with self-employment.

Another tip: When you receive additional income, add it to your investment account rather than spending it all. This is a key principle to building wealth fast, without extra work.

♦ *Maintain a healthy body*—Take the time each day to exercise. Stick to a regular exercise routine. Join a health club or spa, if you can afford it. Play sports with friends or relatives. I run every morning for twenty minutes or so, and I play basketball with friends three times a week. My wife needs the discipline of a skill development program, so she figure skates. A friend of ours uses an exercise bike, catching up on the business news on television at the same time. Assess your own personality to decide what level of formality your exercise program should have, and then stick with it.

Avoid smoking, use alcohol in moderation, maintain a low-fat diet, and take vitamin supplements. Drink plenty of water. Take a few minutes to meditate daily, and, as we do in this book, set aside a day each week for a mental and physical change of pace. Take a vacation from time to time. By following this simple advice, you will feel better, work better, make better investment decisions, and live longer to enjoy your money.

♦ *Have quality medical care and regular medical checkups*—The older you are, the more important this advice is. Develop a good relationship with a family doctor who understands you and your needs. Keep up on the latest medical information. If you don't have a regular physician, you will find yourself in the emergency room when illness strikes, being attended by doctors who are trained more to treat trauma than disease.

Don't overlook your dental care. Professional cleaning twice a year will prevent painful gum disease and tooth decay. I know too many people who finally get to the point where they can afford to eat anything they want, only to find that their teeth or their bodies can't tolerate much more than mush.

♦ *Keep a pet*—Studies have shown that people with pets live longer. Caring for a pet, like caring for a child, keeps you motivated and thoughtful of others.

♦ *Be safety-conscious*—Accidents are the fourth leading cause of death. Avoid life-crippling automobile accidents by buying the safest cars, equipped with airbags and antilock breaks. Avoid high crime areas. Install a reliable security system in your home. And watch your step!

The Best Sources for Health Care

Health care is all the rage these days. My newsletter publisher, Tom Phillips, now publishes three health-related newsletters. You might find one of them useful:

♦ Dr. Julian Whitaker's *Health & Healing* ($69 a year) has more than 500,000 subscribers. He focuses primarily on how older Americans can keep healthy and use the best drugs, surgery, and other treatments for diseases and illnesses. He speaks to sellout crowds wherever he goes.

♦ Earl Mindell's *Joy of Health* ($69 a year) specializes in good nutrition as the gateway to optimal health.

♦ Dr. Marcus Laux's *Malibu Natural Health Letter* ($69 a year) emphasizes natural health methods. He is the director of programs at the Malibu Health and Rehabilitation Clinic.

In my mind, health care is ultimately a personal decision, not one to be decided by the government. I've tried to maintain good health throughout my life by avoiding smoking, alcohol, and coffee, exercising regularly, and eating nutritious meals. I hope to be around a long time as a financial writer and economist.

ACTIONS TO TAKE ON DAY 10

1. Start a regular exercise program.

2. Begin writing down all the food you eat, including when and where you eat, until you have an accurate history of your eating patterns. No exceptions. This is the simplist "diet" plan I know, and it really works.

3. Take vitamins each day. A daily vitamin pill is a cheap plan for starters.

4. Drink plenty of water.

5. Subscribe to a health-oriented newsletter, or read the health columns in the newspaper.

Here's a toast to all of you—to good health and a long, prosperous life.

DAY 11

CUT YOUR COST OF LIVING WITHOUT CUTTING YOUR STANDARD OF LIVING

This may well be our longest day. We will be covering a lot of ground, because the suggestions in this chapter contain the secrets to living like a millionaire without actually being one. I'll show you how to buy just about anything at the best possible price. I'll tell you how to buy your next car at the best bargain price and how to make money again when you sell it. These are the financial secrets that have made the people who have used them financial celebrities. And the best part about it all is that anyone can do it. I use these strategies as if they were second nature. Why? Because they work!

Obviously, I don't expect you to use all of these tips today. But you can become familiar with them today in anticipation of future spending needs. Meanwhile, there may be something on the list that you are contemplating purchasing right now. In that case, reading today's chapter could save you hundreds of dollars or more.

We seem to be conditioned as a society to pay more in order to get more. Pay the most to get the best, right? That philosophy may seem logical, and to a certain extent it is true. In fact, tapping into this belief is the way many successful corporations make their money. They know that if their product is packaged and advertised with all the right bells and whistles and then a "sale" tag is applied to it, most people will believe it is the best quality and the best price, and they won't think twice before buying it. Why waste time shopping around and investigating alternatives when you already "know" what's best? The most common excuse I hear for not shopping around is that it's not worth the time or the hassle. Yet I believe there is another reason for accepting the marketer's word on quality: many people don't know what to ask when they do shop around. They are often intimidated by their own lack of knowledge about the product, and consequently allow salespeople and advertisers to act as their experts. Unfortunately, ignorance isn't bliss; it's costly.

Refinancing Your Home

Let me give you two examples of how much of a "hassle" it was for two of my friends to save thousands of dollars after I spent some time with them.

Michael and Wendy bought a house in the historic district of Orlando, Florida, four years ago. They paid $80,000 for the home and financed it over thirty years at 10 percent. It was a good deal. Property values in Orlando skyrocketed in the ensuing decade and now their house is worth about $165,000. But the last time I ran into them they were complaining about how tight money was. They had just had a baby, which was costing money for day care, clothing, medical treatment, and the like.

Adding to their worries, their second car was a total lemon and in the shop all the time for expensive repairs. They could see only one solution: Sell their house and use the money to buy a smaller, cheaper home and replace the car. Of course they would have to move into a lesser neighborhood, but at least they would reduce their monthly costs.

In some situations, this solution would be the right one. There are times when downsizing is right, especially after children start leaving home and the hassle of maintaining a large house becomes a burden. But Mike and Wendy faced the opposite scenario. They were just beginning their family nest, not watching their little birds fly away, and their need for a large home would expand with time. Moreover, as their children grew, living in a good neighborhood could make the difference between being able to use the public school or having to pay the tuition of expensive private schools. In the long run, the decision to sell their home would have been a foolish and expensive one.

It would have proved to be an unnecessary one, too, in light of the solution I suggested to them. In late 1993, mortgage rates had dropped into the mid 6 percent range. By refinancing their house at lower interest rates, I told them, they would not have to move, and the reduction in their mortgate rates would give them enough extra to buy a better car and even invest a little.

Their first reaction was disbelief. They couldn't understand (or did not want to understand) the simplicity of their situation. For some reason, they had a mental block for numbers or finance—like many people do. It was almost as if refinancing was something menacing or demeaning. Mike was put off by the prospect of having to pay closing costs again. Wendy was unhappy about having to "start over" with a thirty-year mortgage. Funny, but she would rather start over with a thirty year mortgage on a new house, or continue paying more than she needed to for another twenty-six years, rather than "waste" the four years of payments they had already paid.

A few weeks went by and we invited them over to dinner. They were still suffering from the "misery of adulthood and responsibility," as they put it. I could not help but bring up the topic of refinancing again. They didn't want to talk about it, so I let it go. But the next day Wendy called me and asked about the numbers again. They hadn't changed—in fact, the rates were even better. They had the opportunity of reducing their mortgage payment by hundreds of dollars per month. I asked her why she called back, and her response flattened me.

"Mike says it's just too much of a hassle to refinance," she confessed. "The points, appraisal, financial statements, and everything. But I think it's really because he's intimidated by the bankers. He's embarrassed to have to say that our payments are too high, and he doesn't know what kind of paper work they'll need."

My response was, "So you think it's less effort and expense to sell the house?" Then I explained to her exactly how a refinancing works and assured her that the bank officer would walk them through the whole process. "People do it all the time," I reminded her. "Smart people, that is."

A week later Mike and Wendy called back to say they had decided to refinance after all. They had found a lender who offered them a 7 percent mortgage with only one point, reducing their monthly payments by 30 percent. Theirs was a hassle I would have loved to have!

As it turns out, there are millions of Mikes and Wendys in the United States today. Only about 15 percent of homeowners have taken advantage of the historically low rates of interest today to refinance their homes. Many people are simply intimidated by the prospect of facing a loan officer directly and telling the bank what they want. They would rather continue to make high payments, or even turn everything over to a real estate agent and sell the house, than initiate a refinancing. How about you?

We'll talk more about reducing your housing costs and other ways to cut costs without reducing your standard of living later today.

But first let me share with you the story of the financial whiz who can't get a good deal on anything. Whatever he tries to buy, be it airline tickets or a car, he always pays more than he needs to. At least that's the way I see it. His problem is that he doesn't look for an alternative price for the same product. I don't mean that he should buy a lower quality product. On the contrary, I find that the highest quality products provide the best value. My recommendation is simply this: Always look for another supplier of the same product before you sign a contract. Let's get back to my friend and two of his recent purchases.

Purchasing a New Car

The first was a new car. He was looking for a luxury car and already had his heart set on spending $40,000. He was on his way to the dealer when he called to tell me he would pick me up for lunch in his new car. I told him to stop by my house first. I wanted to save him some money. We could worry about lunch later.

I sat him down to drum some sense into him. Buying a new car, I told him, is one of the most expensive lessons you can learn. Buying a new luxury car—from a car dealer no less—is an even more expensive lesson. The more expensive a car, the higher the markup, that's just how it is. The dealers figure that if you can afford to spend $40,000 on a car, what's another $2,000? And they're right. Most people are actually embarrassed to dicker over the prices on expensive cars. They feel that it's beneath them to suggest that a price is too high. Remember the old saying, "If you have to ask the price, you can't afford it"? Sales personnel in luxury businesses use this attitude to intimidate their customers all the time. Don't worry about offending the salesperson or about what he might think of you. You're buying a car, not a character reference for the local country club.

So what should you do? First of all, get out of the showroom! I have yet to understand the allure of buying a car brand new, only to watch its value drop by 20 percent or more the minute you put more than twenty miles on the odometer. What is the point? Why not buy the car with a few thousand miles already on the odometer, and add a few thousand dollars to your pocket? Will it reduce your standard of living if you buy a slightly used car? Will your friends and neighbors stone you? The answer is a resounding no!

Of course, there is a feeling of pride that accompanies the purchase of a brand new car, along with that unmistakable new car smell. But that feeling wears off quickly, and you can get the "Nu-car" air freshener spray when you drive through the car wash. Remember, this is a lump of metal and plastic on rubber wheels that we are talking about, not flesh and bone. I love cars as much as the next person. In fact, I used to own several sports cars—and sank a lot of money into maintaining and driving them. It was an expensive lesson, but well worth the cost. I have realized that a car can be everything I want it to be—but I don't have to pay full price or even near full price for it.

After explaining all this to my friend, he agreed! But then he became even more tentative because he knew that he would have to spend several hours instead of two or three looking for a car. I told him that I would accompany him and give him some tips. At the end of the day he bought a used model of the exact car he was searching for and it cost him $18,000 less than the dealer's sticker price! Not a bad return for a few hours of shopping. Of course, the savings on a mid-size car would be less dramatic, because the markup on luxury cars is so high. Still, the savings are available at any level for those who are willing to put in some extra effort.

The difference between the new car and the one he bought? Each had all the options, the same body style, and an extended warranty for 100,000 miles. The only differences were that his car had 15,000 miles already on it and had been built early in the model year rather than at the end. For $18,000 I'll take a car built in January any day.

Wheeling and Dealing—
Insurance and Your Financial Liability

Even before you or your family gets behind the wheel of a car, you have the potential of a million dollar liability. The political and legal systems have made it possible for people to retire early, thanks to accidental injuries. Fraud and litigation have become a business—a very lucrative one. You must protect yourself first and foremost from this liability. If you feel that your current portfolio is not big enough for anyone to go after, you're wrong. Anyone can sue, and anyone is worth suing.

Often the "best deal" on insurance is the worst deal to get. You want to cut costs on insurance but you mustn't cut corners. It would be easy for me to advise getting the lowest coverage on your auto insurance that your state allows, and I could look good by saving you hundreds of dollars in the short run. But such a recommendation would be wrong. The state does not come to your rescue when you are facing a sympathetic jury about to award a half million dollars to an accident victim. That's usually the domain of bankruptcy judges! The only coverage that you might consider skimping on is collision coverage on an old vehicle that you have decided is not worth repairing if it is damaged in an accident. But comprehensive injury coverage is a must.

Often the companies that offer the superdeals are not so super when it comes time to pay. Cheap insurance is no bargain if the company resists honoring your claims or hassles you when you have an accident. Stick with well-known, reputable companies, and purchase adequate coverage. Increase your coverage to at least $250,000 or as much as $1 million, depending on your circumstances. This may seem extreme, but the extra cost is minimal compared to the safety net that it provides. After all, you must realize that your insurance coverage protects other members of your family who use the vehicles as well. And unless you plan to supervise their driving at all times, you had better be covered. I have found that GEICO and USAA offer the best value in quality automobile insurance coverage. But unless you have a stellar driving record, you can forget about GEICO.

Lower Your Bill without Sacrificing Important Coverage

There are still, however, two sure ways of reducing your insurance bill. The first way is by raising your deductible. Raise it to the highest amount you can afford to pay for a minor repair from a fender bender or vandalism. For example, if your auto insurance deductible is currently $100, raise it to $500 or even $1,000. This move will not only reduce your insurance premiums, it will make you a more cautious driver.

Raising your deductible, moreover, will keep you from filing little claims that notify your insurance company of all your little fender benders—and possibly causing them to cancel your policy. Many insurance companies will cancel your policy if you have two claims in a twelve-month period. The wise person saves insurance for true catastrophes and reduces his insurance premiums in the process.

The second way to reduce your insurance bill is by obtaining coverage for your homeowners insurance and your auto insurance from the same company. You may save up to 10 percent on your total bill. It's like buying in bulk. The insurance company is able to spread its risk among all your policies and reduces its paperwork as well.

Additional discounts are available for certain drivers who are viewed as lower risks. Call your agent to see if you qualify for any of the following discounts:

- ◆ good student—make sure your kids take advantage of school driving programs
- ◆ student away at school
- ◆ carpool to work
- ◆ passive restraints—airbags are the top choice
- ◆ antitheft alarms—the ones that are activated automatically as you lock the car get the highest discount

♦ female, aged 30-64—insurance companies' analyses indicate that women are safer drivers

♦ senior citizen

Reducing Your Cost of Transportation

As I mentioned earlier, used cars offer the best deals in transportation. Restrict your search to cars that are less than two years old with fewer than 25,000 miles. At this age and mileage level it is easy to obtain the best financing terms. The older the car is, the higher the cost of financing will be. The reason for this is that the bank can sell newer model cars more quickly in case of default. This is an important point, because banks are actually a source for buying cars, too. They often have an inventory of cars that have been repossessed.

Taking Advantage of Formerly Leased Cars

These days an excellent source of low mileage, well-maintained cars is formerly leased vehicles. With the heavy push by auto makers to sell cars through any means possible, leasing has become a hot alternative to buying. Many of the larger manufacturers are beginning to experience a huge buildup in inventory as the leasing craze continues. These off-lease cars, cars that have been returned after twenty-four months, are piling up on dealer lots. In order to sell the cars, the manufacturers have been offering special deals that include extended factory warranties regardless of the mileage on the cars.

By purchasing an off-lease vehicle you can avoid paying for the depreciation that will knock around 20 percent off the car's original sticker price. And since the dealers need to sell these vehicles to make room for trade-ins, the bargains can be even better.

Rental agencies are another good source for a used car. Most people reject this idea because they immediately think of how they treated the last rental car they rented. The kids threw up in the back, or Dad kept shifting like a race-car driver, or someone dared to see if that RPM needle would really go past the redline. Sure there are horror stories that follow rental cars. But now that insurance isn't automatically included, most people use their own insurance to cover their rental cars, and consequently they drive rentals even more gently than their own cars. Moreover, rental agencies have their own service departments that keep their cars well maintained. A used rental car is in fact one of the best-maintained used vehicles. It must perform well, or the rent-a-car company will suffer. One of my wife's favorite cars was a Volvo station wagon she purchased from Hertz. It had just over eight thousand miles on it and cost just under $9,000, and it drove like a dream.

Most of the large rent-a-car agencies have a facility through which they sell their rental cars. These cars seldom have more than 15,000 miles on them and will sometimes come with a factory warranty still in force. As with any auto purchase, I suggest that you have it checked by your automotive repair shop first. Check with companies like Hertz, Budget, and Avis to get the lowdown on rental car sales. As a side note, you should consider renting the model of car you want to buy first, to test drive it for a weekend. This will most definitely give you a better idea of what you are getting.

Should You Buy or Lease your Next Car?

If you are really strapped for cash, then leasing is an alternative. What are the advantages? These days, for very little money, you can appear to be the proud owner of somebody else's car. Leasing has become so popular that almost every dealer offers some kind of leasing program. Thanks to factory incentives, the dealer can get you a lease for much less, sometimes up to 50 percent less, than if you were to buy the car.

Advantages of Leasing

- ♦ The monthly payments are lower, because you don't retain any equity.

- ♦ If you use the car for business, part of the lease payment is deductible. (No interest on a personal loan is deductible.)

- ♦ The sales tax is spread out over the term of the lease. Some states add an extra usage fee similar to a sales tax in addition to the normal sales tax.

- ♦ The down payment is lower than that needed for a purchase. Sometimes dealers offer a "no down" deal, but charge an acquisition and disposal fee.

- ♦ It conserves cash (although you build no equity).

- ♦ It is a short-term consideration, giving you the option of changing cars easily when your circumstances change. Popular leases today run for twenty-four to thirty-six months.

- ♦ You can drive a more expensive car than you could if you were purchasing, because you are giving up any equity consideration.

- ♦ If you are disciplined enough, you can invest the difference between your monthly lease and the amount your purchase payment would have been.

- ♦ You have the luxury of driving a new vehicle every two to three years.

Advantages of Buying

- ♦ You retain some equity in the purchase after it is paid for.

- ♦ If you use a home-equity loan, the interest is fully deductible.

- ◆ Buying a used car is usually cheaper than leasing.

- ◆ There are no mileage restrictions. Leased vehicles usually are allowed 12,000 to 15,000 miles annually, after which you are charged a per mile fee. This amount is paid at the end of the lease term. For example, if you have a three-year lease with a 15,000-mile annual allowance, you will be charged for each mile over 45,000 miles at the end of the lease.

- ◆ Lease payments never stop, while loan payments are usually completed within three to five years.

- ◆ There are no charges for excessive wear and tear. On a leased vehicle, you can be charged an extra fee if the car is returned showing rough use or abuse. Remember, when you lease, the car is owned by the dealer, not by you.

My assessment: Buying is preferable to leasing. When all is said and done, leasing is more expensive than buying. You pay a price for the convenience, luxury, and lower monthly payments. You should buy the car, finance it for no more than thiry-six months, and own it free and clear for the rest of its days. Then, after the car is paid for, continue making the payments—to your investment account. The next time you need a new car, you will have the money in the bank, and you can pay cash. Moreover, by owning the car outright, you have a liquid asset at your disposal instead of a perpetual liability through leasing. If you can't pay for a car in thirty-six months, then you can't afford the car, and you should look for something more reasonably priced. Satisfying a craving for a "hot" car that you can't afford, or wanting to compete with the Joneses, can make you worth less and less, not more and more.

COST OF LEASING OVER LIFETIME VS. COST OF BUYING

Assume car costs $15,000

Buy six cars in lifetime—keep for an average of seven years

Use depreciation schedule, buy a used car

Lease fourteen cars, keep for an average of three years

Figure in acquisition fee of $450 and down payment of $1,500

Total capital spent in leasing vs. buying

Difference invested at 8 percent = the real cost of buying vs. leasing

Buying a Car at Auction

Vehicle auctions are another way to buy cars well below their retail price. Auctions are offered by banks, police, and federal agencies. Most people are afraid to buy from auctions because of the shady reputation that auctions have gained over time. You are right to be wary of buying from an auction, but that does not mean you should avoid them altogether. To tell you the truth, I feel safer at an auction with my mechanic then at a used car dealer with his mechanic.

Auctions are usually the domain of used car dealers. This is the place that the true economic value of a car is determined. There is usually no predetermined reserve price at a car auction; the price is determined solely by how much the buyer is willing to pay. Where else do you have the possibility of really being able to buy something at the absolute lowest cost? Even if you don't buy at an auction, attending one can be a valuable source of information to use in your negotiations with the person or dealer you do buy from.

Bidding Up Your Wealth

Probably the most common and overused phrase floating around about finance is "there is no such a thing as a free lunch." For the most part this is true. But sometimes, you can get away with a free lunch and confound all the economists. You just need to know where to look. Buying a car at an auction is an excellent example of the potentially free lunch. Here is what I mean: Because the auctioneer has no predetermined reserve price, you have the possibility of enjoying a car at a cost that is so low, you can actually resell it and make a profit. This isn't a fantasy, it is a reality every day in every part of the country. Just find an auction, follow the steps I've outlined below, and you're on your way to buying a "free" lunch with your profits.

Your daily newspaper holds the key to the best car deals in America today. So sit down in your comfy chair and pull out the Sunday classified section. There are two sections to browse through in particular. The first is obviously the section for cars. The second is the legal section that announces the auctions.

All vehicles are commodities. Their values increase or decrease based on demand, as reflected in their price. An antique or collectible car will sell for ten, fifty, or a hundred times its original cost because there is someone willing to pay the price, hence the demand.

The trick here is to exploit the inefficiency in the market and buy the right car at the right price. What is the right price? If you're like most people, you don't know what the right price is—yet. This is understandable, considering there are so many different price variations on a single vehicle. First, you have the MSRP, or the manufacturer's suggested retail price. That's usually the price that the dealer starts negotiating from. Then you have trade-in value. That's the price you always feel unhappy about when you leave the dealership.

The next batch of prices come from automobile guides. The National Automobile Dealers Association (NADA) Blue Book value (the dealer's guide for wholesale prices), the NADA Yellow Book (the retail prices that customers pay), and the Pace guide show both retail and wholesale prices. These are established values, standards if you like, that automobile dealers have created. They take into account supply, demand, depreciation, historical resale values, and options. But these next two values are the most important.

The first is the auction value. This is determined strictly by demand and is found at the highest bid. It could be $300 for a $15,000 car or it could be $50,000 for a $10,000 car. It depends on how knowledgeable the bidders are.

The second value is the private value. It is filled with emotion. A divorce sale with hard feelings might net you a luxury car for pennies... just to get back at the spouse. You may find a classic car that is worth thousands, but the seller is unaware of its value and willing to let you have it for pennies on the dollar. The seller may need cash quickly to finance another purchase and will let you have a car for a low price. There are literally hundreds of opportunities to get a great deal on a private sale. A great deal is a deal so good that a car can be resold right away or in a few months at a profit. So, scan the paper and make a low bid for any car you like. Remember, the worst that could happen is that the selling party will say no. The best result could produce a "free" car —one that will actually make you money.

Cash Is King, and Good Timing Helps, Too

The wrong time to sell a car is during a recession. The wrong type of car is usually a luxury or sports car. But it's only the wrong time for the sellers—not for you, the buyer. When times are tough, deals abound. To capitalize on these deals you'll need cash or a source of cash. A low interest credit line is ideal. You can borrow from it relatively quickly in order to pounce on a good deal. This is important because the good deals disappear fast. The ability to say "Sold!" and produce the money immediately will put you leaps and bounds ahead of the competition.

Know the Ropes

New and used car dealers buy and sell cars for a living. That's all they do. That's their edge. I don't expect you to become an automobile expert overnight, but there are some cheap ways of getting ahead of the crowd and playing on a level field. You have a distinct advantage over car dealers in that your purchase is a final sale. The dealers are middlemen, and if they pay too much, they won't be able to sell for a profit.

Buying a car for a low price depends on the initial value of the car. The first tool you need is a copy of the NADA guide. Get the Blue Book, not the Yellow Book. The Blue Book contains the wholesale prices while the Yellow Book contains only the retail prices. This publication is the dealer's bible. It lists almost every make and model of car, plus options and any special features. It lists the average retail and wholesale prices paid for cars sold throughout the country.

Another guide that I often recommend is the Pace Buyer's Guide. It costs only $4.95 and contains the wholesale and retail values, options, and the original factory cost of cars.

Dealer Double-Take

At auctions it is sometimes possible to buy a car at 50 percent to 70 percent below its wholesale value. But this is highly unlikely unless there are only a few bidders, or the car is a real

MONEY TO BURN?

Year	Model*	Price New	Value today**	Loss
1993	Saturn	$11,875	$10,700	10%
1993	Acura Integra	$16,950	$11,850	30%
1993	Honda Accord	$18,245	$12,925	33%
1993	Ford Taurus	$17,775	$11,550	36%
1993	Olds 98	$24,595	$15,075	39%
1993	Audi 100CS	$32,900	$20,000	39%
1993	Ford Tempo	$12,800	$ 7,625	40%
1993	Pontiac G/P	$21,635	$12,600	42%
1991	BMW 750i	$74,000	$25,750	42%

* Fully loaded model
**Source: Pace Buyer's Guide

lemon. Most often you will be able to purchase the vehicle at 20 percent to 40 percent below its wholesale value. That is why many dealers frequent public auto auctions. They know that they can turn over a good car bought from an auction and make a healthy profit. You can follow the same pattern.

Buy a car at an auction if you can get it for at least 30 percent under the NADA wholesale value. If you are interested in buying and selling the car for a profit, then you must buy and sell the car in the same year. This is important. If you bought a 1991 Acura Legend in January 1992 and sold it in January 1994, the car would be three years old. But, if you sold the car in November 1993, it would only be two years old and you would get a better price, even though January 1993 was only two months away. This is part of the psychology that is involved in the car game. It could mean an extra $1,000 in your pocket.

Winning Tips for Auction Success

♦ Emotions often run high at auctions. Wanting to show that you are the best man at the card table often leads to mistakes. You aren't looking for a dream car to keep, but a bargain car to sell. Don't get emotionally involved with the auction. Remember that your aim is to buy low and sell high—not buy high and hope!

♦ It is essential that you take a mechanic to the auction preview. It might cost you $50 an hour on Saturday at the auction house, but it is money well spent. Have a few cars lined up that you are seriously considering— this will save you money by reducing time spent browsing for a car. Always go to the preview early and ask the mechanic to join you later, an hour or so before the auction. Most good auction houses will allow you to start the car up and check under the hood. A good mechanic can spot telltale signs that you

may never think about. If the mechanic says it's a
lemon, take his word for it and go on to the next car.

♦ Remember you are looking for wholesale prices, not
retail. Plan to pay only up to 70 percent of the
wholesale value for the car. You can find the wholesale value by checking your NADA guide book.

♦ You've got to act disinterested, but with your eyes
wide open and your trigger finger ready. I recommend you let someone else begin the bidding. If you
begin, the auctioneer and his handlers may try to
sucker you into paying more because you've shown
immediate interest.

♦ You should practice watching the crowd for the first
three or four cars. You will detect a noticeable pause
in the action after the first few rounds of bidding. The
time to get involved in the bidding is when it slows
down. Don't be intimidated if the auctioneer begins to
make disparaging remarks about the lack of bidders or
the low price. He is there to sell and will try to evoke
any emotion he can to get the best price. Jump into
the bidding when it begins to slow down, so there are
only two other bidders in the ring with you. Be calm.
Only bid up to your 70 percent limit, including the
buyer's premium, the amount the auction house adds
on to the winning bid as its commission. The buyer's
premium is usually 10 percent or less.

A No-Lose Situation

The day after you have bought your car at auction, put an ad in
the local paper or "Auto Trader." Price the car at just under the
average retail value specified in the NADA handbook, so you have
the advantage of advertising the car at "below NADA book value."
That statement alone will attract a few customers. Turn it over

quickly, lock in a profit of 30 percent or more, and then go back to the auction house to start over. If you want to, use the car for a while before selling it, but make sure that you have it up for sale at least two months before the end of the year, before the new models have come out and your car has aged another year.

Another Source: The Federal Government

Another source for low cost vehicles is the U.S. government. The U.S. Customs Service and the IRS often hold auctions for items that have been seized or confiscated. The auctions are held by a company called EG&G Dynatrend, which is the sole contractor for the U.S. Customs Service. Take this opportunity to buy items far below wholesale prices. You can subscribe annually for nationwide auction locations for $50 per year. Regional guides cost $25 per year. To subscribe, send your name and address and the region you wish to subscribe to (east, west, or nationwide) along with a check to EG&G Dynatrend, 2300 Clarendon Boulevard, Suite 705, Attn. PAL, Arlington, Virginia 22201. To hear a complete recording of services and upcoming auction locations, call 703-351-7887.

If You Don't Like to Buy Used...

If you have your mind set on a new car or you just don't believe in buying anything used, you can still benefit by following a few simple steps:

♦ Never buy a car the first time you see it. Americans tend to be emotionally attached to their cars and they often make impulsive decisions to buy them. Car dealers will always find a way for you to afford them, even if it means extending your payments beyond five years. After all, you are making the payments, not them. I remember seeing ads from car dealers three years ago offering $20,000 cars for $99 per month. In addition to a hefty down payment, the small print showed that buyers would be making these little payments for over twelve years! Be careful not to jeopardize your long-term financial goals for the sake of short-lived vanity. Before you go off to the dealers, calculate exactly how much you can afford to pay and over how many months. Make sure each dealer gives you a complete price, written on his letterhead. If they won't do this they obviously have something to hide. This also signals to the dealer that you are serious about shopping around, and he or she will be more likely to give you a rock-bottom price. Spend a couple of days thinking about your purchase and the different cars and dealers you have spoken to. Only after you have checked with several dealers are you ready to make your purchase.

♦   Learn the actual price the dealer paid the manufacturer for the car. Most dealers will accept a profit of anywhere from $200 to $500 over their cost. To find their cost, you have several options today that weren't available just five years ago. Several services will provide you the actual cost the dealer paid for the car, including any options you may want. The breakdown is so precise, that they show you the cost of each option and the actual dealer markup. The markup can be astounding. On one car I checked for a friend, the CD player was a $2,000 option, yet the dealer's cost was only $400. These buying services will send you a complete printout on as many cars as you want, for a relatively small fee. Most services will provide the details for under $20 per car. I recommend using *Consumer Reports* buying service. You can get more information about this by contacting them at Nationwide Auto Brokers, 17517 West Ten Mile Road, Southfield, Michigan 48075. Nationwide

Auto Brokers Service provides a similar service; call 800-521-7257.

♦ Dealers will always try to sell you on two things. The first is credit life insurance and the second is a warranty. Both are important, but chances are you already have one, and the other can be bought for less through other reputable sources. Credit life insurance protection pays the balance of your car loan if you die, thereby protecting your heirs from becoming responsible for your loan. Two things can be said about credit life insurance. As sensible as it sounds, you don't need it. And as affordable as it sounds, it probably costs too much. You have a choice—use your money to make yourself wealthy, or use your money to make the insurance company wealthy. For this service you pay a fee that usually adds up to between 8 percent and 10 percent of your car loan amount over forty-two months. It is a waste of money, pure and simple. Even if you don't have life insurance (which we will talk about later today), you can still buy an inexpensive term-insurance policy to cover the value of the automobile loan. A term policy on a $20,000 loan will cost about $40 the first year. Each succeeding year, both numbers will be lower. Just say NO to credit life insurance!

The second offer is a warranty from a dealer. Where warranties are concerned, it pays to do your homework. I personally believe that a warranty is valuable on vehicles. A single repair can pay for an entire warranty many times over. But I also know that dealers overcharge by 100 percent and more when it comes to warranties. How do I know? Because the same warranty can be purchased from a reputable company for less than half the price most of the time.

When it comes to negotiations, let the salesperson know that you are aware that extended warranties are a source of huge profits to the dealer. The best way to make your case is to contact another warranty source ahead of time in order to get a price. Many insurance companies now offer extended warranty coverage. GEICO and USAA, which I mentioned above in the section on insurance, both offer this service. Another independent source is General Electric, which underwrites many of the dealers' own warranty services. Use this information to negotiate a lower warranty price with the dealer, or simply buy your warranty coverage from one of these outside sources.

Use Public Transportation

One final suggestion on reducing your cost of transportation is to use public transportation whenever you can. The savings over owning and operating a car are absolutely phenomenal. Unfortunately, most parts of the country don't have a good, safe system of mass transit. But if it is available, use it. Depending on where you live, you could save between $2,000 and $3,000 by not owning a car. If you must have a car for recreational purposes, then consider owning just one car instead of two or three.

Is Your House a Money Pit in Disguise?

Over their lifetime, people spend hundreds and even thousands of dollars on gambles to make themselves wealthier. Lotto tickets, Vegas-style junkets, "Get Rich Quick" schemes, and the like are just what you think they are: too good to be true. But if you knew absolutely that you could win a $100,000 payoff, guaranteed, by purchasing a certain lotto ticket every month, would you do it? Of course you would. Well, you may be sitting on a gold mine that could garner you thousands of dollars and you don't even know it. To cash in on it, you will need one tool that is very inexpensive but most effective: the discipline to buy that "lotto ticket" every month. If you're a homeowner, you're already a potential winner—no further purchase required, except your monthly "tickets." The mortgage papers and deed for your house are your potential sweepstakes—so start playing now!

How does it work? Let's suppose that you have a thirty-year mortgage at 9.5 percent. You just made the first payment and are facing another 359 more. Your monthly principal-and-interest payment is approximately $840. At the end of the thirty-year term you will have paid a whopping $202,707 in interest alone. But, if you are disciplined enough to buy the lotto tickets I am about to describe to you, you can cut that amount in half and put $100,000 in your pocket—and even more, if your own mortgage balance is higher.

You can start as soon as your next payment is due. Contact your mortgage company and tell them you want to make accelerated payments toward your principal. They may have some forms for you to fill out. Then when your next payment is due, write a check for $990 instead of $840. Do the same thing every month for the next seventeen years. For an extra $150 per month you just knocked thirteen years, over one-third of your working life, off your mortgage. Your home will be fully paid for, long before you retire and in time to start paying your children's college tuition.

The Adjustable Rate Game

If you've ever been sold a home by a real estate agent, the idea of adjustable rate mortgages will somehow come up. They're not a bad deal, but they are definitely not for everyone. In fact, more than two-thirds of mortgages are fixed rate products.

Adjustable rate mortgages will help you keep the payment on your house lower for a while, sometimes for a long while. They are pegged to an index rate, such as the one-year treasury bill rate. Every year the mortgage is adjusted to that rate, usually to a maximum of two percentage points in either direction. For example, let's assume that you started an adjustable rate mortgage at 4.5 percent, and the one-year treasury bill rate was at 4 percent. The terms of your mortgage allow the rate to be raised once a year by a maximum of two percentage points based on the change of the one-year treasury bill rate. The maximum you can ever pay, according to the contract, is 10.5 percent. In the meantime, your rate will fluctuate each year, but never by more than 2 percent.

If you had chosen a fixed rate mortgage instead, your monthly payment would have stayed the same throughout the life of the loan. Most people choose this plan because it is less risky. But that stability comes at a price: fixed rate mortgages always cost more than adjustables, usually two full points or more.

Even though they are more risky, the savings on adjustable rate mortgages are so high in the first few years that it takes a long time and a high inflation rate for a fixed rate mortgage to save you any money. It may be years before you catch up with an adjustable rate deal. Meanwhile, an adjustable mortgage will give you extra money to increase your monthly contribution to your investment account. In general, unless you plan to stay in your home for more than ten years, I recommend an adjustable rate mortgage.

Can You Afford a Home-equity Loan?

While on the subject of homeownership, I think this is a good time to bring up how I feel about second mortgages and home-equity loans. They are playing an increasingly important role in peoples' lives, and I don't really think many of you grasp the seriousness of this type of financing.

Home-equity loans and second mortgages were originally designed as ways to borrow money for home improvement—which would in turn add value to your home. But, since the phase-out of the personal interest deduction, home-equity lines of credit and second mortgages have been widely advertised as sources of low-cost loans for all purposes. The tax deductibility of interest is a strong selling point.

Home-equity loans and second mortgages are loans secured by the equity in your home. They are the easiest loans to obtain. Lenders know that the last loan or debt a homeowner will default on is one tied to the home. In addition, if the borrower does default, the lender has the home as collateral. The terms for home-equity loans are usually as favorable as those for home mortgages. Sometimes they are even more favorable. Home-equity loans are usually variable-rate loans that are pegged to the prime lending rate. Second mortgages are usually fixed-rate loans.

Affording a home-equity loan goes beyond simple number crunching. It is a matter that should be given very serious thought. Although home-equity loans are very attractive and an easy source of cash, the consequences of default are much more serious than those associated with default on an unsecured loan. The difference between the risk of default on an unsecured loan, such as a credit card, and the risk of default on a secured loan, such as a home-equity loan, is referred to as the risk premium. It is the difference between the rates of the two types of loans. Sometimes it is advisable to pay the higher rate for an unsecured loan, even if a home-equity loan is available.

Home-equity loans and second mortgages have the following advantages:

♦ low interest rates

♦ flexible payment schedules (usually five-year, eight-year, and ten-year maturities)

♦ zero or low closing costs—many lenders will charge less than $200 for the whole loan process

♦ low qualification standards—your home equity is security enough.

♦ deductibility of interest (on the home-equity loan)

- ◆ short approval time—again, the lender is backed by more equity than debt

- ◆ usually no prepayment penalty

- ◆ availability

- ◆ flexibility—home equity loans are available as lines of credit or straight loans

And the following are the loans disadvantages:

- ◆ the danger of foreclosure if you default

- ◆ ease of availability—they're so easy to get, you may overlook the dangers

- ◆ low qualification standards—the lenders only care about your equity, and if you don't pay, they will foreclose and probably make more than your original debt.

- ◆ restriction of your credit—home-equity lines of credit are sometimes counted on your credit report as loans regardless of whether you have drawn upon them

- ◆ prevalence of scams that advertise easy loans but charge very high rates

- ◆ the lien that is placed on your house

You should use a home-equity loan or second mortgage for home improvements that will add resale value, or you should apply the money to any venture that will yield growth or income.

If you are considering a home-equity loan or second mortgage, you should "lock in" a home-equity credit line, when interest rates are low. The interest will not begin to accrue until the funds are used. This way, you can have a low-cost source of funds for future home improvement—but remember, even if you don't use it, the credit line will still show up as a debt on your credit report, and a lien will be placed on your home.

Safety First

I'm not against using a home-equity loan as a source of financing, as long as you have all the bases covered. To use the loan as an extension of your credit facility is not a good idea. Buying a car is a good way to put a home-equity loan or second mortgage to use, but only if the loan is used as additional financing. Always maintain a 10 percent margin between what the car is worth at wholesale prices and what you owe on it. For example, if you buy a $10,000 used car that is worth only $9,000 at wholesale, borrow only $8,100 through a home-equity loan or second mortgage. The main point is liquidity. Always be in a position to make payment on your home-equity loan or second mortgage, by selling the asset, if necessary. If you aren't in such a position, you are living dangerously.

One way to make certain that you can pay off your home-equity loan or second mortgage is to have enough available credit to do so. For example, make sure you have $10,000 in available cash from your credit cards, as a safety measure, before you take out a $10,000 home-equity loan or second mortgage. Even though the interest rate would be monstrous, at least you will have the resources to pay off a secured loan with an unsecured loan not tied to your house. Take this route only as a last resort, as a way to buy time. Remember, you still must pay back the credit card company, or face bankruptcy.

Do not use a home-equity loan or second mortgage to pay for the following:

- ♦ vacations and getaways—you will still be paying for a trip tomorrow that you took five years ago

- ♦ consolidation of your credit cards; unless you have the discipline not to use your credit cards again, you will end up with twice the outstanding credit—and no more equity to fall back on

- ♦ investments in stocks or bonds (unless you have the

money to repay the loan in case your investment heads south)

♦ income taxes—once again you are paying for an expense that should already be paid; a home-equity loan should not be a bail-out tool

♦ everyday expenses regardless of their nature— home-equity loans are not income, they are debts

The Best Use of a Home-equity Loan or Second Mortgage

The best use for a home-equity loan is as an investment in a money-making business. Taking out a home-equity loan and investing the funds in your own home-based business, for example, has many potential benefits. You provide expansion capital to get the business going. You can loan the money to your business at an interest rate higher than the one you're paying (at the market rate) on your home-equity loan. By investing in your own profitable business, you also ensure that all the money will be repaid. Just make sure it is a money-making business. Don't borrow money to invest in an unproved business. Use a home-equity loan preferably for additional capital, not original capital.

DON'T TRIP OVER TERMINOLOGY

The home-equity loan and the second mortgage are similar concepts. There is a difference, however. A second mortgage is a lump-sum payment to you. Interest begins to accumulate immediately, regardless of when you actually use the money.

A home-equity loan is like a line of credit. Once it is established, you can draw from it as long as you have credit available. You pay interest on the loan only when you begin using the borrowed funds.

In either case, consider whether you want to mortgage your house for the short-term satisfaction of taking a vacation or paying off a couple of credit cards. I know of too many people who have lost all their equity through indiscriminate borrowing and then entered their retirement years with no place to live and nothing to live on.

The Wrong Life Insurance Can Kill You—
Financially Speaking

Today, life insurance serves two useful purposes: one for when you die, and one for while you live. When you die, the life insurance company pays a lump sum to your beneficiaries, the people who have counted on your income to provide part of their livelihood. While you live, tax-deferred insurance products such as annuities and whole life and variable life plans can be extremely valuable for conservative estate planning and should not be overlooked as investment opportunities.

Today, however, we are talking about expenses, not investments, and particularly about how you can cut your expenses to the bone. If you want to reduce the cost of simple death protection, term life insurance is much less expensive than whole or universal life. The reason is quite simple. With whole life, you build up equity in your policy. But that equity costs money, making your premiums much higher than they would be if you were only purchasing death benefits. With term insurance, on the other hand, you are not building up any cash benefit, so you don't have to contribute to the investment portion of the policy. Term insurance is a bare-bones policy at a bare-bones price. The difference between the premiums for a whole life policy and a term life policy can propel your portfolio far ahead of any returns the life insurance companies might pay you.

There will be a time when investing in modern life insurance products will make sense for you. Perhaps you are in that situation now. But if you are just starting your investment program, you would be better off for now buying term insurance and investing the difference in your Automatic Investment Plan. Term insurance is pure insurance—no-frills protection for your family. This is the least expensive life insurance. To save even more, buy annually renewable term insurance or one of the new twenty-year level term policies. Many companies offer deals for new subscribers for the first five years of their policies. Again, shopping around will help you find the deals.

For the best rates on term insurance, contact David T. Phillips & Co., 3200 N. Dobson Road., Building C, Chandler, Arizona 85224, 800-223-9610, 602-897-6088. Phillips is a nationwide independent insurance agency that specializes in getting you the cheapest, best term policies around. The call is free, and there is no obligation. No insurance salesman will call.

The Payoff

Today you have the opportunity to take a huge slice out of all of your expenses and not reduce your standard of living by one iota. The waste, in just everyday expenses, is enormous. The rewards are well worth the extra few hours it might take to identify and act upon possible opportunities. Look at it this way: you're willing to spend an hour driving back and forth to a discount grocery store to save ten or twenty dollars. Why not spend the next hour looking over your spending habits and save hundreds or even thousands of dollars? It is that simple, and it is that effective.

The payoff from this exercise is not only financial. By taking the steps that we've gone over today, you'll find that you have become a disciplined spender, ready to question what the establishment is throwing at you. Will you ever buy credit-life insurance again? I doubt it. The next time you look for a car, you will automatically look at how much money it is really worth and how much you can save by spending an extra few days to locate a used model.

The payoff begins to expand tremendously when you realize that you are passing on your knowledge to your children and other family members. That is the key to prosperity and financial freedom for generations to come.

ACTIONS TO TAKE ON DAY 11

1. Consider refinancing your home at a lower interest rate.
2. Prepare to save thousands on your next car purchase: Buy used!
3. Buy term insurance—and invest the difference.
4. Look for new ways to cut waste from your budget.

NEVER BUY ANYTHING WITHOUT
DOING THIS FIRST...

To find the right bargains, each day, the first thing you should do is consult the classified section of your newspaper. If there is an item that you need, new or used, there is a good chance you will see it advertised in the newspaper. And the price will most likely beat any store. Why? People have been conditioned to sell for less when they advertise in the classified section. Most people are in a hurry when they use the classifieds. They have a short window of opportunity, just the three days that the ad will run, and they don't want to risk losing a customer. Often they feel embarrassed about selling something that they once paid the full retail price for, and now don't use, don't want, and can't afford. Finally, most classified users also think they need to discount heavily in order to make up for their lack of credibility in not having an ongoing business.

A Story You Won't Believe

You can put this understanding of human nature to work for you. Those who understand the classifieds market can clean up on these poor chumps who are ready and willing to give away merchandise at abnormally low prices. The classified section of most newspapers is a huge free market economy. I like to browse through the classifieds, especially on the weekends, just to get an idea of which yesterday's must-have items have become today's white elephants. I'm always amazed at the number of people who advertise a product as "never been used" or "still in the carton" for 50 percent to 70 percent off the retail price—computers, golf clubs, exercise equipment, VCRs. You can save hundreds of dollars on these big-ticket items.

You just never know when you will see a huge financial opportunity staring you in the face. You may have heard of the person who saw a Mercedes Convertible offered for sale for $25. At first he thought it was a typo. Lots of other browsers probably did, too. But after thinking about the ad all day, he finally called the number. "Is this for real?" he asked. To his amazement, it was. The seller was involved in a messy divorce. Her husband had run off with his secretary, telling his wife she could keep the house if she would just sell his Mercedes and send him the cash. She sold it all right—but at a price that would garner her husband almost nothing.

Whether this story is true or apocryphal, it illustrates the crazy motivations some people have for selling their possessions through the classifieds. And you can cash in on that craziness. More important, thousands of people use the classifieds just for the heck of it. Among these advertisers are a huge number of impulse sellers, people who sell just because they feel like it at the time. They may need the garage space or some ready cash. Or they may just be tired of seeing the item staring them in the face, reminding them of the impulse purchase they made in the first place. Their mistake can become your golden opportunity.

Why Bother?

Why bother with all of this? What use is it to spend time poring over classifieds and other sources for good deals? Why not just go to the store like everyone else? If you want to be like everyone else, that is your right. But everyone else spends time worrying about how to make the next mortgage payment, or how they will put their kids through college, or whether they will be retiring young or not at all. Everyone else is prone to live life according to what's on their plate. Those who take the time to form a foundation find that they are well ahead of everyone else and in charge of their own destiny. Saving money by looking through classifieds is just one small way of doing that. Remember, of course, that spending, no matter how much you "save," never improves your bottom line. But spending smart can keep you from damaging your financial health. And as we all know, an ounce of prevention is worth a pound of cure.

Some people I talk to consider their spare time too valuable to spend hunting for bargains. Phrases like "it's not worth my time," or "my time's too valuable for that," are commonplace in our society. This may be true for low-priced items. But does it make sense to overspend by $200—perhaps twenty hours of your labor—when five hours of careful shopping could have netted you a bargain price?

Stacking the Deck in Your Favor... Completely

I remember the first time I saw a computer. It was the size of an elephant and just as slow. This was the future of the modern home? No way, most said. Too big, too slow, too expensive.

Obviously, they were wrong. If you are not part of the computerized generation, then you need to hurry up and join. We are heading into an age where the majority of financial and trading functions will be available at home via the personal computer. And the best thing about it is its low cost. Today you can buy an entire home system from computer superstores like Computer City or Radio Shack for as little as $800. Or order one from a computer magazine directly from the manufacturer and save a little more. Better yet, go back to the classifieds. You can often find a late model computer, never used, for half the retail price.

How can a computer help you reduce the cost of purchasing merchandise? Much like the classified section of the newspaper, the computer is now a giant global marketplace that communicates over the phone lines. Using on-line services (programs that allow computers to execute certain functions) such as CompuServe, America On-line, Prodigy, and so on allows you to search the world for what you need. Each one of these on-line programs offers a section called "forum" and a classified section. The forums are question-and-answer platforms that allow you to communicate with another user or group of users all over the United States and the world. These forums are invaluable sources for answers to almost any imaginable question, from advice on which paint is the best to use at home to a review on just about any type of vehicle.

The classified section affords you the opportunity to buy and sell any goods, much like your local newspaper. You simply place an ad in the system with a description of the item and your computer's special account number for responses. The only difference is that your responses are much quicker and your audience is in the millions instead of just thousands.

The Value of On-line Services

On-line services should not be restricted just to classifieds and forums. They are also an excellent source of investment research, travel planning, educational services, and a host of other resources that you once would have had to spend hours on the phone or at the library to obtain. They are a way to reduce your cost of living by legitimately saving you time and money.

On-line investment services can also provide you with the lowest-cost brokerage services available. Most services allow trading on any listed stock or mutual fund available, including international securities that trade in the United States under the form of American depository receipts (see page 208). In addition to brokerage services, you can also conduct in-depth research on most of the companies that trade on any U.S. exchange. This includes annual reports, earnings projections, news releases, insider buying and selling of securities, charts for price and volume, historical information, and much more. Most will even keep track of a model portfolio, updating prices automatically. All you have to do is enter a few keystrokes to track your success.

On-line travel services are also very impressive. You can pull up the same screen your travel agent can see. Find the lowest price tickets to any destination, and book the ticket yourself. The airlines have a deal with the on-line service to mail the tickets directly to you, or you can pick them up from the airline's ticket office. The travel services also allow you to compare hotel and car rental services worldwide, even providing specific descriptions of hotels and their facilities.

My favorite on-line service in CompuServe. It carries no advertisements that slow down competitors like Prodigy, and the information I have retrieved from it has always been up-to-date and accurate. It costs $14.95 for the basic service. Additional services have per-minute charges that vary by the service. However, many services are covered at no extra charge under the monthly fee. There are no long distance telephone charges as the on-line service companies have set up local call facilities in almost every city. To get more information on on-line services contact the following today:

♦ **CompuServe** quick on-line connection, easy referencing, and information on lodging, car rental, visas, advisories, currencies, and restaurants. Price for service, which includes some travel services, is $14.95 per month for the basic service package. They often offer specials for new subscribers, so be sure to ask about these before signing up. It is menu driven, not graphics oriented. Another advantage is that you can "talk" by computer with other people before making your choice. Large networks of electronic conversation groups are springing up around the country and the world, and you can cash in on their knowledge simply by getting on line with them. For more information contact CompuServe, P.O. Box 20212, Columbus, Ohio 43220; 800-848-8990. (Their lines are often busy—keep trying!)

♦ **Prodigy** offers similar services as CompuServe. It costs $14.95 per month and is accessible through a network of local numbers. Prodigy is driven by a combination menu/graphics package. Because of the constant graphic displays and advertisements, the service is very slow. For more information contact: Prodigy, 445 Hamilton Avenue, White Plains, New York 10601, 800-776-3449.

♦ **America On-line** offers the first five hours of service for $9.95 per month and charges $3.50 per hour thereafter. The service is not as comprehensive in its optional features as either CompuServe or Prodigy. The service offers menu/graphic interface. For more information contact America On-line, 8619 Westwood Center Drive, Suite 200, Vienna, Virginia 22182, 800-827-6364.

♦ **GEnie** offers a variety of different packages. In addition to its $8.95 per month off-peak service charge, you are charged $9.50 per hour during peak usage times, and $3.00 for nonprime time usage. For more information contact GEnie, 401 N. Washington Street, Rockville, Maryland 20849, 800-638-9636.

Equipment

All the services operate on DOS. CompuServe and America On-line are planning to introduce Mac early this year. Prodigy and GEnie offer Mac and DOS. The higher a service's bites per second (bps) modem speed the faster you can receive information. Each service supports modem speeds of 300 bps to 2,400 bps. CompuServe, Prodigy, and GEnie also offer 9,600 bps to selected locations.

Warning

One final word of caution is in order regarding these electronic communications networks. Many unscrupulous persons get involved in forum groups and make friends with those on line. These are still strangers, not acquaintances, and you should not get involved on a personal level. Additionally, much pornographic material unfortunately drifts through the lines. If you have children at home, or even at college, you should beware of the potential dangers involved in allowing them to become conversational buddies with complete strangers.

Travel for Less—Much Less

Traveling is usually a financial headache for most people. The fare wars are never fair. The few cheap seats that are available are usually scooped up before you even dial a number. The best hotels are too expensive. Rent-a-car companies jack up the price with insurance premiums and high mileage charges. Exchange rates are always working against you. Sometimes the best part of many vacations is going back home.

It doesn't have to be that way. Hundreds of good deals are available to satisfy any budget. You just have to know where to look. Your vacation may not be any better, but it will definitely cost you much less—and that always makes my vacation seem better!

♦ *The classifieds—where else?* Often the lowest fares
are in the newspaper, sold by individuals whose travel plans have changed and who want to salvage some
of their nonrefundable purchases. Tickets usually sell
for 50 percent to 75 percent off the regular price.
But, you should be aware that it is against airline policy to travel on someone else's ticket. This is because
the Department of Transportation requires the airlines to submit a true manifest of passengers for each
flight. On domestic flights, airlines are pretty lax
about enforcing this rule, and the market for cheap
third-party tickets flourishes. It could get you into
trouble, however, so think twice before doing it.

♦ *Package deals*—When you're visiting friends or
family who are providing you with a place to stay,
you don't usually think of purchasing a travel package. But these packages provide such good deals that
you can often come out ahead, even if you don't use
all of the package. Especially if you are visiting a
major vacation spot, look into a fly/drive/hotel package. These package deals are put together by tour
operators in volume. They usually include great
deals on hotels rooms, car rentals, and airfare for
about half the cost of each item if booked separately.
Your travel agent has a long list of fly/drive packages,
or, once again, check the travel section in your Sunday newspaper. As a bonus, the packages often come
with discount coupons for meals and attractions as
well. Let someone else have the headache of reserv-
ing an entire vacation for you. Hint: be flexible with
the dates and hotel locations. Most of the time you'll
be staying with friends or family anyway, so choose
the cheapest package. Your main goal should be the
cheap airfare and rental car. And if you can get a

hotel room besides, why not use it? Your hosts may be more appreciative than you would expect.

♦ *Fare wars*—Get a guaranteed cheap seat by purchasing tickets during fare wars, even though you may not use the ticket for several months. These are normally nonrefundable, but a great deal is like money in the bank. After the fare war you can change the date of travel for up to a year for a $25-$35 change fee on most airlines—frustrating, but still a bargain if your fare is low enough. Cheapest days to schedule travel are Tuesday, Wednesday, and Saturday. During major holidays, best days for arrival and departure are the actual holiday—Christmas Day or Thanksgiving Day, for example. You can still get there in time for dinner—and save hundreds of dollars too.

♦ *Discounts*—Request discount coupons and special fares in writing from the customer service department of rent-a-car companies, airlines, and hotels. Tell them you've used their product before and are a loyal customer or, alternatively, that you are trying it out for the first time. For best results send them a request in writing. By spending $10 in postage and paper, you will receive discounts worth hundreds of dollars. These companies want your business and have tons of specials lined up just for your asking. Call their 800 numbers, usually listed in the phone books, and ask for the company's customer service, public relations, or administrative offices address.

♦ *Affinity cards*—Affinity cards with travel savings such as the AA Advantage cards from American Airlines can prove to be a source of huge discounts. But, you should consider three important factors before acquiring a card:

1. The annual fee is usually very high, between $50 and $75. If you don't use the card, then you're paying too much in fees.

2. You must use the cards a lot to enjoy the benefits. They usually give you one free mile for each dollar of purchase. Most freebies don't start until your five-thousandth mile. In addition, the interest rate is usually much higher than any of the cards I recommend on Day 24—between 15 percent and 19.8 percent. Unless you can pay your balance off in full each month, you're heading for financial trouble with these high rate cards. It's cheaper to buy a discount ticket in most cases.

3. A word of caution: The only people who truly come out ahead with this type of card are the disciplined spenders who have a strong aversion to interest payments. By using the card for everything from gasoline to groceries, you can really add up the miles. I have always advised against using credit cards for regular purchases and groceries—unless you pay the balance in full, each and every month. The best way to use the card for regular purchases without finding a huge surprise in your statement at the end of the month is to deduct the purchase from your checkbook each time you use the card. That way you will keep a running total of your debt, and when the bill comes at the end of the month, the money will be in your checking account, ready to pay it off.

You need to charge at least $10,000 per year for this program to be worthwhile, and that's enough debt to kill most family budgets. Use this "bargain" technique only if you are extremely self-disciplined, enough to maintain the same wise spending patterns you had when you used only cash.

ACTIONS TO TAKE ON DAY 12

1. Get in the habit of reading the classifieds—starting today.

2. When you plan your next trip, take advantage of discounted airfares.

3. Plan ahead. When you are pressed for time, bargain hunting goes out the window. Always be aware of your future spending needs, and be prepared to buy a bargain when you see it.

4. Search for alternative sources. The classified ads, computer networking services, and package discounts are just a few possibilities.

DAY 13

CUT YOUR TAXES TO THE BONE

Today we are going to talk about taxes. But this time it's going to be fun, because instead of telling you all the taxes you have to pay, I'm going to teach you how to keep your taxes low and how to reduce them even further. Let's get started.

Live in a Low-Tax State

First of all, consider living and working in a low-tax state. The Tax Foundation keeps up with which states offer the lowest state and local tax burden. There are several states that qualify as low-tax states:

♦ Texas has outstanding tax incentives to new businesses and individuals. Texas has no individual or corporate

income tax, while maintaining reasonable sales and
property taxes

♦ New Hampshire is the only state in the union that
has neither a sales tax nor an individual income tax

♦ Nevada has no state income tax and is booming eco-
nomically

♦ Florida is a popular state for retirees, with no individual income tax

♦ Several border cities take advantage of dual state tax
havens, e.g., Vancouver, Washington, takes advantage of no income tax in Washington, and no sales
tax in Oregon.

If you get a job offer in any of the state tax havens, consider
moving.

Home Ownership—Your Easiest Tax Shelter

Home ownership is one of the best tax shelters still available for
average taxpayers, no matter where you live. Not only can owning your home be a source of enjoyment and pride, it can be your
personal money machine. As a homeowner you can deduct the
cost of interest of your mortgage against your personal income. In
the first year of owning a $90,000 home, that can mean an extra
$2,500 in your pocket, just from deducting the interest. Throw in
the property tax deduction, and you'll cut another $300 or $400
from your bottom-line federal tax bill if your property tax is about
$1,200. If your property taxes are higher, your deductions will be
higher as well. And if you are in the highest tax brackets, your savings will be even greater. To get a rough idea of the amount that
you will benefit from your home, multiply your tax rate by your
total deductible home expenses. This includes interest, property
taxes, and other financing costs such as points. Suddenly that
mortgage doesn't seem so expensive!

Whenever you sell a personal residence for more than you paid for it, you can defer the taxes on the profit if you buy a new house of equal or greater value within two years of the sale. For example, if you bought a house for $80,000 and sold it for $140,000, you might owe as much as $25,000 in capital gains taxes ordinarily. But if you have personally resided in the house for three of the previous five years, you won't have to pay tax on the $60,000 profit. You simply roll the profit over into the equity of your new home. Just be sure to buy another house within two years, with a purchase price at least as high as the sales price of your previous home, and you will have no current tax consequences, regardless of how much money you use as a down payment.

This is a tax deferral method, not a tax exemption. Eventually all that rolled-over equity will have to be taxed, either when you decide to buy a smaller, less expensive home, or when you sell your real estate altogether and move into alternative housing—a rented condo, a grown child's extra bedroom, or a travel trailer, for example. But another ruling in the tax code eases the pain of your eventual capital gains. After you reach age fifty-five, you can sell the home and keep any profits up to $125,000 free of taxes, as long as you have lived in the house for three of the previous five years. Unfortunately, you can only use this capital gains exclusion once. This exclusion can save you as much as $50,000, depending on your tax bracket, and even more, when you consider that you have been able to use all that money to invest in larger, more expensive homes, instead of sharing your profits with Uncle Sam along the way.

So, if you are set on buying a house instead of renting, you can ride the tax deduction train for quite a while and then get your profits out of your house without paying any tax. The deductibility of interest is the best reason to make the smallest down payment possible on a house—if, that is, you are able to make the monthly payments. The more you owe, the larger your tax benefit.

You may, however, be uncomfortable with having so little equity in your personal residence. After all, this is more than an investment, it's your home. Two methods can help you build equity while still taking full advantage of the interest deduction. First, you can use your tax savings to invest in a separate investment account. You will sleep easier, knowing you have the capital to pay down your mortgage, should your financial situation change. The Automatic Investment Plan (AIP) described in the first week works perfectly for this.

Another strategy is to use the accelerated payment technique that I showed you yesterday to pay off your mortgage early, that is, in seventeen years rather than thirty. That way, you get the highest tax savings during your peak earning (and thus peak tax rate) years. Then, when your income and your tax rate both slow down because of retirement, your house is paid for. You win on both counts!

Pension Plans: Good for Workers and Bosses

Whether you are self-employed or working for someone else, you can increase your wealth dramatically by establishing one or more IRS-approved pension plans.

The importance of these tax shelters is twofold. The obvious advantage is tax relief. The money you set aside in your IRS-approved pension fund represents an immediate reduction in taxable income and thus an immediate reduction in your current tax bill. The second and most important benefit derived from a pension fund is the tax-free compounding of your investments. These investments can grow tax free until they are withdrawn, increasing your overall return by an extra 15 percent to 36 percent. The tax deferral can mean the difference between a prosperous retirement and a retirement fraught with uncertainty and insecurity.

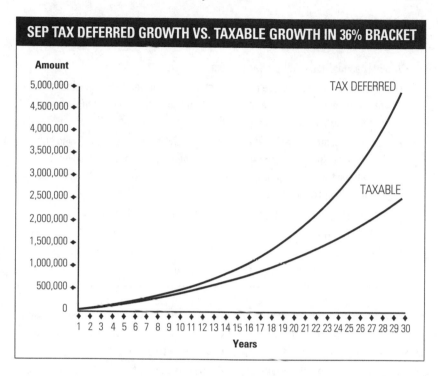

SEP TAX DEFERRED GROWTH VS. TAXABLE GROWTH IN 36% BRACKET

Simplified Employee Pensions—
The Super Individual Retirement Account

Simplified Employee Pensions (SEP) provide retirement income for business owners and their employees. SEPs are similar to Individual Retirement Accounts (IRAs), but better. You can contribute up to 15 percent of earned income, to a total of $30,000 annually. By contrast, a regular IRA can shelter only $2,000 annually. The employer can also contribute additional amounts to the accounts of employees, at his discretion, through company matching programs. These contributions are also tax deductible.

The base percentage of income contributed must be the same for employers and employees; you cannot use this plan to shelter your own money without sharing it with your employees as well. Moreover, contributions cannot be limited to just one or two

---

SIMPLIFIED EMPLOYEE PENSION—A CLOSER LOOK

A SEP is an individual retirement account in which:

1. Employer contributions are made under a definite formula that specifies the requirements an employee must satisfy to share in an allocation and how the allocated amount is contributed.

2. Employer contributions must be made to the SEP of each employee who has reached the age of twenty-one, and performed service for the employer during at least three of the immediately preceding five years and received at least $385 in compensation.

3. The employer contributions cannot discriminate in favor of highly compensated employees.

4. The employer cannot prohibit withdrawal by employees. The employee owns the money the day it's put into the plan.

---

employees and the owner. They must be made for all participating employees, including part time or seasonal help. Farsighted business people see the personal advantage to providing retirement benefits for employees, as employees who are treated well tend to be more loyal and hardworking as well.

The best part about SEPs is that there are very few headaches from paperwork. There are no lengthy or complex IRS or Labor Department forms. The accounts are managed by financial institutions such as brokerage firms, banks, and mutual fund families. The cost to set up an SEP is less than $200. Most brokerage firms and banks can set the plan up for your company.

Are You Overpaying?
The Benefits of an IRA

Every year you may be overpaying on your taxes. Why? Because you aren't taking advantage of the laws designed to help you reduce your taxes. Your final tax bill is calculated on the basis of taxable income. That may seem very straightforward: Just look at your gross salary, and pay the tax. But your taxable income is the amount of income left over after your standard or itemized deductions. The main goal in tax planning is to reduce your taxable income and thereby reduce the amount you pay in taxes. Admittedly, the loopholes are getting smaller and harder to find. But some do remain.

The IRA is a great vehicle to use in reducing part of your tax liability. The contribution acts as a tax credit, reducing your taxable income dollar for dollar if neither you nor your spouse has another pension plan. Even if you do have a pension plan or other qualified retirement plan, you may still be eligible for the dollar-for-dollar benefit, if your adjusted gross income (or AGI, the gross income minus deductions) does not exceed $25,000. If you are filing a joint return, the figure is $40,000.

Owe Less Today, and Owe Less Tomorrow

The IRA is meant to be a tax-deferred retirement vehicle. All the contributions to your IRA and the gains from investments made within your IRA grow tax free until you withdraw them. Only when you begin withdrawing funds from your IRA, at age fifty-nine and a half or more, will you begin paying taxes on the withdrawals. For most people, this means paying taxes at a much lower rate, because taxable income logically falls at retirement.

Compounded Profits, Tax Free

Your IRA shields your investment income from all taxes, allowing you to make an extra 15 percent, 28 percent, or 31 percent on the money in your IRA account, depending on your tax bracket. Tax-free compounding can have a huge effect on the growth of your wealth. Look at the following graph to see the difference between tax-free growth and taxed growth:

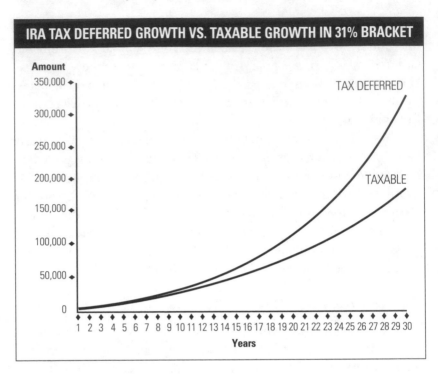

Contribute Anyway

Do you already have a pension fund? You can still contribute to an IRA, no matter what other retirement plans you have. You won't be able to deduct the contribution amount from your taxable income, but the benefits of tax-free compounded growth within the account will still make it worthwhile. You'll pay less at withdrawal time, too, since the principal portion of your IRA will already have been taxed.

How Much Can You Invest in Your IRA?

If you are a typical worker, you can invest up to $2,000 annually in an IRA. Your working spouse can also invest $2,000. If your spouse is not employed, he or she can invest up to $250. You can make contributions to the IRA at any time during the year—daily, weekly, monthly, or in a lump sum. You have until

April 15 of the current year to make a contribution for the previous year. For example, you have until April 15, 1996, to make a contribution for 1995.

Invest Early and Often

The sooner you invest, the sooner you can enjoy tax-free growth for the whole year. If you wait until April 15 of the following year, you're just giving money away. Use your Christmas bonus or your tax refund check to make a lump sum contribution. Or, if you don't have the entire deposit at once, start out at $50 a week.

Don't let the money in your IRA lie idle. Put it to work for you right away. I recommend that you invest in several diversified-stock mutual funds. Investments in the financial markets can often earn 10 percent or more a year over time, but you must be patient. Some years will be good, others not so good. Occasional years will be great!

Don't Fall into the Tax-Free Trap

Don't direct your IRA funds to a tax-sheltered investment. This defeats the purpose of an IRA. Remember, the IRA is already tax-sheltered. Stay away from tax-exempt government/municipal bonds and tax-free mutual funds- -both tax-sheltered investments—where your IRA is concerned. You can invest in tax-free mutual funds or tax-exempt government/municipal bonds within your regular savings or your AIP.

Double Your Advantage

If you open your IRA before April 15 you can double your advantage. You can invest for the previous year and for the current year at the same time, doubling your contribution and your deduction. You could invest up to $8,000 at once if you meet all the qualifications. That's a nice chunk of change to put to work.

Investigate the fees charged by the IRA trustee you are considering, the organization that will administer your IRA. Many institutions can administer your IRA, including banks, brokerage houses, and qualified guardians such as retirement managers. Fees for IRAs range from nothing at all to hundreds of dollars. If you're planning to invest in the stock or bond market, keep your IRA at a discount broker. The annual maintenance charge should be less than $35. Charles Schwab & Co. offers a no-fee IRA for account balances of more than $10,000. Schwab & Co.'s phone number for IRAs is 800-435-4000.

Lowering your taxes is as good as money in the bank—your bank. There are many ways to reduce your tax burden and increase your financial freedom. Unfortunately, many people either don't know about them or are too lazy to use them. I can never understand why anyone would not taking advantage of legal opportunities to pay less in tax. According to the Constitution, taxes are meant to be voluntary. We all know that this statement has been turned into a farce, but I for one will volunteer as little as I am legally obliged to.

Following are some ways that you can participate in the pursuit of lower taxes.

1. Contribute the maximum possible to your company-established 401k plan. This is a self-defined plan, meaning that you direct the investment of your money from a choice provided to you by the plan administrator. I am shocked by the lack of employee participation in these plans. This is like free money. If it doesn't go in your plan, it goes right to the government. Yet many people, intimidated by something they don't completely understand, let this opportunity pass them by.

There is a limit to how much of your income you can contribute to the plan, usually a percentage of your gross income that is determined by your plan administrator according to government guidelines. The maximum amount is adjusted for inflation each year. In 1993 the amount was approximately $8,900; in 1994 it was about 3 percent higher, or $9,200.

This contribution is taken right off the top of your paycheck, before your federal tax is figured. Consequently, your tax bite will be lower, so your take-home pay will not shrink by the full amount of your contribution. Better still, because this works like an automatic savings plan, you won't even realize that it is gone.

Best of all, your company might even contribute to the plan by matching part of your contribution and making lump sum payments as a bonus to all employees. Normally, you have to be a plan participant (vested in the plan) for three to five years in order to keep what the company contributed. If you leave the company before this time, the amount contributed by the company will remain in the general fund.

If your company plan is set up in a certain way, you can even borrow from your plan at a market interest rate in order to finance some other purpose. Borrowing this money from yourself comes with a beneficial twist: the interest you pay on the loan goes right back to your own account. The money you use to buy your car, for example, is tax sheltered. And the money that you might otherwise have used to buy the car is now also earning interest. But I must warn you: If you quit or lose your job, you will have to repay the whole amount immediately to avoid paying a penalty on the amount outstanding, in addition to income taxes. Consequently, I don't recommend borrowing from this plan unless you have assets you could sell to replace the money.

2. Be sure to deduct any interest paid for investments. Although personal interest, such as that charged on credit cards, is no longer deductible, investment interest is. If you borrow for investment purposes, the interest is fully deductible against any investment income. Other tactics include the following:

♦ If you are the sole proprietor of a business or rental property, be sure to deduct the tax preparer's fee on your Schedule C (business) or E (rental property) instead of on the Schedule A. On a Schedule A, you have to meet the 2 percent floor for miscellaneous deductions.

♦ People often overlook charitable contributions simply because they don't think of them. Yet these are probably the easiest to document. Property contributions, such as furniture or clothing donations, should be recorded and deducted.

♦ If you cash in a certificate of deposit early and suffer a penalty, the loss is deductible.

3. Miscellaneous deductions can add up. There is a 2 percent floor for them, which means that any amount over 2 percent of your adjusted gross income is deductible. If you are taking the standard deduction, however, the miscellaneous deduction section does not apply to you.

Here are some often forgotten miscellaneous deductions:

♦ union dues and assessments

♦ small tools, safety equipment, and other job supplies

♦ safe-deposit box fees

♦ fees paid to a tax advisor to prepare your return or represent you during an audit

♦ dues owed to professional societies

♦ investment-counselor fees and investment-service costs

♦ certain travel and lodging costs incurred while seeking employment

IRA: A Quick Review

As the most accessible form of retirement planning for most people, the IRA is the most important place for most people to begin their tax planning. Begin contributing to your IRA immediately. If you haven't set one up, call your broker, or Charles Schwab, or even visit your local bank. The forms are very simple and require only a few minutes to fill out. Don't delay. The power of tax-deferred compounding is a huge force, working while you are awake and while you are asleep.

1. Contribute money to your IRA. Until April 15th of each year, you can make a tax deductible contribution to your IRA that will reduce your tax burden for the previous year. More important, it will also allow you to take advantage of tax-deferred growth. The following qualifications must be met before your IRA contributions can be considered tax deductible:

- ♦ If you're single or married and you and your spouse maintain separate IRAs, your contribution limit is $2,000 each. If your spouse is not employed, you can contribute a total of $2,250.

- ♦ The money contributed to an IRA must be earned, based on your salary, self-employment income, commissions, tips, and so forth. Income from rent, interest, dividends, pension distribution, or Social Security does not qualify. According to the IRS, these are sources of unearned income!

- ♦ If you participate in a company-sponsored plan that gives you tax breaks (e.g., a profit-sharing or pension plan), you cannot deduct your IRA contribution unless your adjusted gross income is less than $25,000 ($40,000 for couples).

- ♦ But, the IRA contribution is still partially deductible if you are single, covered by a plan, and your adjusted gross income is between $25,000 and $35,000 or if you are married, you and your spouse are covered by a plan and your joint adjusted gross income is $40,000 to $50,000.

Money contributed to your IRA is for long-term investment. In most cases, if you withdraw funds from your IRA before age fifty-nine and a half, you will be subject not only to income tax on that distribution but also to a 10 percent withdrawal penalty.

2. Even if you don't qualify to make tax-deductible contributions to your IRA, you can still enjoy the benefits of tax-deferred growth. This feature alone makes it more than worth your while. You may make a nondeductible contribution to your IRA regardless of the number of other pension or retirement plans that you have.

3. Don't let your IRA take the place of your AIP. Keep contributing monthly, and use these funds for nonretirement purposes.

ACTIONS TO TAKE ON DAY 13

1. Keep your taxes low.
2. Discover home ownership tax advantages.
3. Find out how pension plans can help reduce taxes.
4. Start your own Individual Retirement Account (IRA).

REVIEW AND MEDITATION

Over the past six days we've tackled some of the most important aspects of financial well-being. I concentrated especially on the basic expenditures you make every month. These are the puddles in Solzhenitsyn's proverb. If you don't take care of them, they will drown you much more quickly than the sea.

I have encountered many people who disregard the daily aspects of finance until it is too late. The purpose of this book, especially of the past two weeks, is to help you incorporate wealth and financial freedom into your daily routine, so that it becomes as normal as waking up. You'll think twice about buying a brand new car now—because you realize the folly of paying too much. The key here is to develop a finely honed sense of value.

Over the course of my career I have met some very wealthy people, most of them self-made. I have noticed one common trait among them. They are conscious of value. This does not mean that they live parsimoniously, with their entire extended family in a one-bedroom apartment, or that they shop exclusively at hyper-markets to save a little here or there. They simply know how to control their spending habits, how to shop around for the best deal, and how to recognize the value of the dollar. They know just how difficult it is to earn a dollar and how easy it is to waste one through a lifestyle of lavish spending. More important, because they have gained control of wasteful spending, they are now able to enjoy a life of generous living, because their financial futures are secure.

Financial Freedom Begins with the Family

The family plays an important role on the path to financial freedom. Without their support and appreciation of what you are trying to accomplish, the task is fruitless. After all, are you not doing this as much for them as for yourself? Yet you might find it difficult to take input from a seven-year-old seriously. But, remember it isn't the child's actual opinion that matters so much as the concept of including the entire family in understanding the acquisition and allocation of the family's resources.

The family can be a source of both strength and frustration. Each person develops a set of financial values, and oddly, mem-bers of the same family may have completely different attitudes toward money. One of our sons is extremely frugal. We never have to tell him that an item is too expensive or extravagant, because he decides that for himself. In fact, he gets more frus-trated with his spendthrift sister than we do, as he tries to make her see how foolish some of her expenditures can be. Trying to blend these personalities to form a family partnership that works for everyone can be a challenging objective, but one well worth the try.

A good friend of mine once told me that he had many arguments with his father about spending. His father took money very seriously, and while he was growing up my friend took money seriously, too—he spent it. He now wishes that he had understood at a younger age what his father was trying to teach him. His dad never worried about money because he had planned his finances so well that he really didn't have to worry. It was not a matter of being rich, but of following a game plan that he had begun with his first job. His father understood at a young age the true value of a dollar, because when you come to your career earning less than one dollar an hour, you begin to understand its value very quickly.

Zeroing in on the Problem

Today we live in a world of zeros. The budget deficit is counted in billions, the stock market is valued in trillions, and credit card companies fill up our mailboxes with offers of thousands. This gives us a false sense of wealth—a sense that we all live in a world of big numbers, and somehow, someday, our bank accounts will also have numbers with lots of zeros behind them.

If you truly wish to succeed with a plan to increase your financial freedom, you must sometimes allow the forceful side of yourself to come forth. Discipline in saving and spending should be the goal for your entire family, and if it takes a few arguments along the way to achieve it—especially with the older college-aged kids—then it must be done. One of the main problems that I see with families that I counsel today is the lack of respect the children and sometimes the spouse have for the value of financial planning. I also see parents lavishing gifts on their children, with the excuse that "they're only young once." It is an attitude that stems in part from the current economic and social environment. It's as if people are saying "so what" about the future—"it's today that counts."

This "live for today" attitude is fine if you only expect to live another few years and plan to work until that time. But with the excellent probability that you will live for twenty or thirty years past normal retirement, you had better make some sacrifices today, so you don't sacrifice your entire retirement instead. It's like the story of Bonnie and Clyde I gave you on Day 3—Bonnie who began investing $1,000 a year for ten years versus Clyde who didn't begin saving until ten years later. Bonnie was able to quit saving after ten years and still come out ahead of her belated husband, Clyde, by $55,000 in thirty years! It pays to sacrifice early, so you can reap the benefits for a lifetime.

The Ulterior Motive

After spending a week going over the nitty-gritty details of budgeting and how to reduce your cost of living without decreasing your standard of living, you should have a pretty good idea of how expensive it is to overlook the little things. The little things can add up mighty fast.

By adopting the ideas we have discussed this week, you have set the stage to take much larger strides toward financial freedom. The extra money that you're going to save each month from your newly refinanced mortgage or the money that you will save the next time you buy a car or insurance or even—perhaps especially—the money you save each time you decide not to stop for a milk shake or another impulse item, must now be put to good use.

The first week we talked about the AIP using mutual funds. Taking advantage of these programs is more important than knowing about them. It's easy to procrastinate, but the results can be dangerous to your financial health. The biggest problem that I see most people encounter is their own reluctance to begin. To them, this newfound information means change. And for some reason, most people feel apprehensive about change.

Take the mortgage reduction for example. It may take you two or three hours to start the process as you find your mortgage papers, look them over for the name and address of the mortgage company, and call a few lenders to find the best deal. It may take a few more hours before you're through, as the lender calls to ask questions and prepare papers. But isn't it worth half a dozen hours to save several thousand dollars? You have no reason to feel apprehensive about that kind of change.

Over the next few days we are going to explore even more ways to increase you wealth and invest it with confidence.

ACTIONS TO TAKE ON DAY 14

1. Look for every way possible to eliminate wasteful spending on transportation, housing, food, utilities, and entertainment.

2. Put your extra savings to good use—invest more in your AIP.

THIRD WEEK:
Increase Your
Income and Investments

DAY 15

GET AN "EASY" RAISE

When was the last time you got a substantial raise in income from your job? I'm not talking about a mere 3 percent or the cost of living, but 10 percent or more?

Because of the current economic climate, technological efficiency, and competition from overseas, many workers feel they will be next to join the unemployment line. Take a look at any business section of the local paper in the last five years, and you will see a headline along the lines of "Company X Lays off 2,000 Employees." In fact, over the last two years companies have laid off almost two thousand workers a day. Sounds pretty worrisome, and the bad news intimidates most employees into feeling grateful for any job, at any salary. Asking for a raise may tip them right out of the boat.

But the truth is, the media tend to highlight only the negative side of "downsizing." They don't report the new jobs being created every day, especially in small businesses and service industries. While one company may be trimming away at excess workers, others are building and hiring. Net employment is actually increasing.

So don't despair. There is a way to maintain your job security and even get a substantial pay raise practically every year.

Adopt a Pro-business Mentality

The first step toward obtaining a raise is to understand business itself. The president of a large corporation once told me, "Only a handful of employees understands the purpose of business." I asked him what he meant. He explained, "Most employees seriously think the purpose of business is to provide jobs and benefits for workers." He went on to say that the employees worth keeping understand the true purpose of business—providing goods and services to sell to customers at a profit. Ultimately, the reason your company is in business today, making a profit, is because it is satisfying its customers. That's the free enterprise system in a nutshell.

Businesses are not charities. While they may do many good works and donate to many good causes, they can only stay in business if they are dedicated to making profits by satisfying their customers. In a competitive world, customers can go elsewhere to get what they want. Executives and employees must be on their toes if they hope to keep their customers.

Your company must make money in order for you to have a job. Otherwise, you will both be out of business. It looks out for its long-term financial well-being. You have to do the same. Besides, getting a raise from your employer may be much easier than you think. But you have to take the first step.

Adopting a pro-business mentality means that you have to see things through the eyes of the company. Its main concern is how to make more money for every additional dollar it spends. It's called efficiency. Today every company is striving for it.

So before you ask for a raise, evaluate your position in the company. How long have you been there? How productive are you? Are you a real asset to the company? How do you rank with other workers, both in terms of productivity and pay scale?

I recently asked the owner of a large 750-employee corporation what he expected his employees to do in order to get a raise. Before he answered that question, he posed another one, "How much is the employee being paid, in relation to other workers?" Then he issued what was in effect another warning, "Never be the highest paid employee in your occupation." It may be great for your ego, but it exposes you to layoffs if the company faces a downturn.

His warning makes sense. As I mentioned above, one of a business's biggest concerns is how to get the most out of each employee for every dollar it spends. Suppose the manager is reviewing labor costs and notices that one bookkeeper, department supervisor, or loan officer is earning half again as much as the others, for whatever reason. That manager is going to look long and hard at the productivity of that highest paid individual.

If you are already at the top of the pay scale for your job description, your job security may be in danger. You may need to ask for a promotion to a position with an entirely different pay scale, rather than a simple raise.

Ask This Simple Question and You'll Get a 10 Percent Raise in One Month!

This leads us to the most important question you can ask if you want to get a raise, *"How can I help make this company more successful?"*

That's all there is to it. Your employer is willing to pay you more, much more, if he can get more out of you.

Notice how different this question is from what labor unions usually demand of employers. Union leaders will insist that their workers get paid more *regardless* of increased productivity. They feel they deserve more because of the increased cost of living or because workers aren't getting their "fair share" of the company's profits. They may have a point, but their methods are often counterproductive. How much smarter to offer a benefit to the employer in exchange for a higher wage!

There is also a good possibility that even if your boss isn't the owner, your paycheck is tied to your performance. He has to get the most out of you in order to make more himself. Executive contracts are laced with bonus and override clauses.

For this reason, your boss will be more than willing to talk with you if you come armed with examples of how you have helped the company grow, save money, or operate more efficiently.

Make a List

Make a list right now of things you have done in the past six months or one year that no one else could have done as well, even if it is something as small as cleaning the coffee pot when it needs it. One woman I know, Dorrie, saved her job and earned herself a promotion simply by bringing a rose to the most cantankerous biddy in the office. No, the biddy was not Dorrie's supervisor, she was simply a co-worker. But you know the type: they get on everyone's nerves, whine and complain, criticize others, but manage to keep the job because they happen to be the fastest and most accurate in the office. Meanwhile, they make life miserable for all the other co-workers. Dorrie has the knack of soothing the ruffled feathers and hurt feelings of the office staff when the biddy starts cackling, and as a consequence, the office manager can spend her time on more important matters. This talent for resolving personality conflicts never appears in a job description, but it's an asset that has given Dorrie immense job security—and has made the work environment more pleasant.

Another fellow I know wasn't the best or the most accurate, but he was the most available. George worked for a large consulting firm, which required a good bit of travel. Most of his co-workers had to plan ahead before they could travel and if family matters interfered, they would beg off. George never turned down a request from the company to travel, and as a result he was considered indispensable. Whenever the company managers talked about downsizing, George's name remained on the "keep" list because sometimes sending anybody, even someone with little experience, is better than nobody. Moreover, because of the additional experience he gained on the road, George's skills improved, and he began making the keep list for both reasons.

Pinpoint the attributes that make you indispensable to your company, and make sure your supervisor is aware of how valuable you really are. Once you have established your job security through indispensability, you will be ready to ask for a raise.

Now you are ready to develop a plan of action with your boss, who will be more than willing to help you succeed, because he is ready to recognize that you make his life easier, more productive, and more profitable.

If at First You Don't Succeed...

There are ways of opening the eyes of your superiors. The old adage "Actions speak louder than words" is another way to approach the situation. If you know certain ways to increase your salability, use them. After all, what you are doing is selling your skills and abilities for more money.

Take the chance that your work will be rewarded. In some organizations this is the way to the top. But there are some pitfalls to this approach, and solutions, that you should be aware of:

- ♦ Don't become a pest. If your ideas are not appreciated or the extra profits you produce are overlooked, step back. Remember, someone will be making a profit from your efforts. And that same someone will be running to ask you for advice. The idea is to give your boss a taste of the champagne, not the whole bottle.

♦ Don't oversell yourself. The last thing you need is a boss who won't reward any of your efforts regardless of how much you make for him or how good you make him look even if you don't deliver all the goods. Leave yourself some margin for error.

I recall the story about the employee who told his boss that he could increase sales in the city's Chinatown district, an area that the company had been trying to sell to for years. He had boasted that he was studying Chinese. But when time came to sell to the area, he admitted that he was still in Chinese 101. Not only did he not get the raise, he made his boss look bad. You can guess the rest.

♦ Avoid becoming a victim of the janitor complex. This is the worst possible fate. Not only will you be unhappy, but you will probably be out of a job. The janitor complex, simply put, is the idea that you are the reason the company is in business. Without you, the company would surely fail. This fantasy will get you into trouble. If your efforts are ignored, then try another tack. Sulking and whining are not the way to financial freedom--persistence and effort are!

♦ Do not try to go over your boss's head. You have to work from within. The last thing you need is an angry, unproductive work environment. If your boss is that hard to get to, then you are probably in the wrong company.

Adopt the Stance of a Warrior

When your livelihood is at stake, which is how you should look at a situation that is getting you nowhere, you need to fight to get ahead. Sometimes it is hard to stomach the idea of finding another job. But if your ideas are not appreciated, you can bet that you're not on the top of your boss's gift list. So, when you are ready to present your idea, you have to adopt the stance of a warrior. You have to cover your flanks by making sure that your plan has no holes in it. Your objective is to make a sale! And the best salesmen know that the secret to selling is being able to anticipate and overcome any objections.

What You Should Do with That Raise

Once you get a raise, you will be tempted to spend it, or increase your standard of living. Consider an alternative. Increase your contributions to your Automatic Investment Plan (AIP)!

You can gain a tremendous benefit by adding to your AIP. Under your current AIP, you may not reach that million dollar figure (or whatever you listed on Day 1) for another twenty years. But by adding an additional 10 percent each month to your account, you have moved your date of celebrating financial independence to fifteen years or less. The advantages to adding to your independent investment account are (1) more funds in your account to work for you and (2) the compounding effect of capital gains and dividends from these additional funds.

It pays to get a raise and invest it!

ACTIONS TO TAKE ON DAY 15

1. Plan on getting a raise (10 percent or more) by answering the following: "How can you make your company (department) more successful?"

2. Make a list of things you have done recently to improve the productivity or environment of your job.

3. Be sure to invest part or all of your raise in an AIP.

DAY 16

MAKE AN APPOINTMENT WITH SUCCESS

The Greek tycoon and shipping magnate Aristotle Onassis carried a little black book with him wherever he went. In it, he wrote the name and profession of every interesting person he met. Later in life he called on many of these people to advise him about building his business. The results were legendary. At the height of his power, the Onassis family was considered one of the richest in the world.

Onassis knew the value of reinventing the wheel. He had seen too many people fail, not because they were innovators, but because they lacked the sense to imitate the success of others when it came to the simple things. He wasn't about to make the same mistakes. You shouldn't either.

Get out a pad of paper and make a list of all the people you know or could be introduced to through friends and family. Identify those who have become successful. Contact each one of them by letter or through another party. Be sure not to call them on the phone. This is too personal and you may catch them at a busy time. You know what it's like to be interrupted by a telephone call from a stranger, but nearly everyone enjoys a short personal letter.

Say in a simple note or message that you want to interview them to get an insight on how they have made their business successful. Probably only a few will respond to your request. But a few is all you need.

As soon as you hear back, call for an appointment. When you meet, you should explain that you are trying to get ahead and would like some help or guidelines from someone who has already made it. Come armed with some knowledge of the person's background, product, and family. This is the ultimate demonstration of respect for a self-made person, and most will be willing to share their techniques quite freely. You see, many successful people thrive on helping others succeed. It is almost a duty they feel to repay their own good fortune. Ego also plays a big part.

Remember the story at the beginning of this book about the millionaire who made money while he was asleep? He was flattered that people came to him to ask about the secret of his success.

If possible, maintain your contacts with the people you meet who interest you. You may have something in common that would allow you to get together on a regular basis. I remember one young man who used to play basketball with me and other faculty members at Rollins College, where I am an adjunct professor. He had a successful business that took a turn for the worse. He lost the business and was unemployed. But all the while he kept in touch with me and others. He still participated in sports with us as always. One day he asked me if I knew of any opportunities in the financial field, which was his field as well. I told him that I had just heard from a good friend of mine whose company was looking for a financial analyst. And, voila! Today, just two-and-a-half years later, he has become one of the top analysts at the company. And you know, he still comes out to play ball.

Six Degrees of Separation

Networking is one of the greatest tools that you can develop. It is a safety net if you ever encounter difficulty. Look at it like this. If you have just ten friends, who have ten friends, and so on, you have access to a great many people. A good movie in 1993 that received little publicity was called *Six Degrees of Separation*. The title meant that only six people that you know separate you from any other person in the world, no matter how famous or infamous that person may be. Think about it.

Networking is like raising a child. If you nurture him and give him attention and respect, the child will help you in return. As Proverbs says, "Raise up a child in the way he shall go, and when he is old he will not depart from it." Just so with your circle of friends and connections. And always be prepared to help someone who comes to you for advice or direction. It may seem like a waste of time now, but it will pay off handsomely in the future. Remember, it doesn't matter how certain your future is now, there will inevitably come a time when you need help. Burning bridges or ignoring the pleas of a friend can come back to haunt you.

Business Never Grows Old

Each person you interview will be able to shed new light on what you are doing or trying to accomplish. If you cannot find the answers you need within your circle of contacts, don't despair. There are many ways to meet and interview successful people outside your circle of friends. Contact local or national business organizations and participate in their social functions. For example, if you are a car enthusiast, you could join a local car club. Other members may be from every walk of life, but they have something in common with you. This common bond will create another contact that might be able to help you. By joining several clubs, you will open many more doors to success. The following are other examples of how you can network at very low cost and receive very high returns:

♦ Contact your local chamber of commerce. It holds weekly meetings of businesspeople in the area for networking. The meeting may have a specific topic that may not apply to you, but the ultimate purpose is to share information and insight.

♦ Contact the local or national Small Business Administration. Its experts can refer you to members who can answer some of your questions at no charge. The members also hold regular meetings to discuss the small business and entrepreneurial environment.

♦ My favorite organization for help and new ideas is the Service Corps of Retired Executives (SCORE). If you are looking for inexpensive business advice that works, look no further than your local white pages. Most communities have groups of retirees who can help or advise you with just about any problem or idea. These advisors are former businessmen, executives, and consultants. They are more than happy to assist you. Usually they will charge a small fee but sometimes they will advise you at no charge. Take advantage of this tremendous resource by contacting SCORE, 409 3rd Street SW, 4th floor, Washington, D.C. 20024, 202-205-6762.

♦ For another inexpensive forum of information, contact your local Better Business Bureau. For more information call 800-564-0001.

It is up to you to attend these meetings on a regular basis. They provide a proven way to get ahead. For the most part, meeting with someone is a low-cost event. And if you don't like someone you meet, you are under no obligation to continue the friendship. People feel much more comfortable dealing with people they know. This applies to bankers as well as baby-sitters. Networking brings truth to the saying that "success breeds success." It's time to become successful!

ACTIONS TO TAKE ON DAY 16

1. Make a list of successful people you know or whom your friends know.
2. Contact successful acquaintances and discover their secrets to financial success.
3. Develop the art of networking.
4. Join local organizations and attend their meetings.

CONTROL YOUR DESTINY

Day 17 is one of my favorite days. After today you will be able to control your financial destiny completely. Have you ever wondered how most of the people on the Forbes Magazine list of the 400 Richest People in America get there? Inheritance, playing the stock market, buying real estate? Not likely. In reality, the answer is they start their own businesses and make them grow.

Probably the most familiar example of a family on this list is the Walton family, founders and developers of Wal-Mart, the largest retail store chain in the world. The founder of Wal-Mart, Sam Walton, died in 1993. But during his lifetime he managed to turn a four-store operation into the biggest retailing giant in the world, surpassing the sales of Kmart and Sears in less than forty years. Most of the growth came in the last ten years.

Everyone has a Sam Walton deep inside them. It is the spirit of entrepreneurship, the will to succeed under your own terms, without being at the mercy of your next paycheck from a company that someone else owns. There is nothing so satisfying as being your own boss, setting your own hours, wheeling and dealing with your own capital, and reaping the rewards of your own efforts. It's something that few people nowadays have—a sense of security.

Of course, a business can go bust just as easily as you can lose a job. But at least in a business it is usually up to you whether or not it will succeed. And if it does fail, you know why. You're the first person to know, not the last on the totem pole waiting for a pink slip.

Today we will look at the various aspects of setting up, owning, and running your own business. It is an exciting and, more important, a profitable way to enjoy your life.

My Own Story

To give you an idea of how exciting starting your own business can be, let me tell you my story.

Twenty years ago I was working as a research analyst for the CIA. The job description sounded glamorous, the benefits seemed great, and the government job was pretty secure. But the work was bureaucratic and wasn't challenging enough. I disliked the nine-to-five routine and wanted to be my own boss.

One day I noticed an ad in a magazine for a book called *Lazy Man's Way to Riches*. I've never considered myself "lazy," but the title intrigued me. Now, thousands of people probably read that same ad. Maybe more. But most of them simply shrugged their shoulders and turned the page. Not I. I ordered a copy, and when it arrived, I read it from cover to cover. Within weeks I had started my first home business, which eventually led to a successful career in the financial world.

Today I am going to share with you the secrets to starting a successful business of your own while limiting your risk and your initial capital investment.

Most people think the first step toward owning your own business is literally to set up shop. Lease a building, hire a secretary and a bookkeeper, buy furniture, install phone lines, and look successful. That's exactly the reason that most businesses fail in the first year. Too much money goes into looking like a business and acting like a business, and not enough goes into testing whether the business can succeed. Here's how I did it. First, I needed something to sell, something that would appeal to customers immediately. My first business was selling five hundred copies of my booklet , which I advertised in a magazine for $3 each. Then I waited for the profits to roll in.

I sold seven booklets.

Yes, my first attempt failed. But I hadn't lost much. My self-esteem was injured, but printing costs had been small and the ad was less than fifty bucks. And I still had no overhead to worry about, so after a few weeks of thought, I tried again with a different product. After my first fiasco, I decided to test the waters before purchasing the inventory.

I placed an ad in the classified section of an entrepreneurial magazine, and this time the orders did start rolling in. My wife and I were excited, but we still didn't start "setting up shop" and we didn't start dressing like millionaires, either. We reinvested all our profits, stored inventory in our baby's bedroom, and filled orders from our kitchen table. All our profits went back into the business, buying larger space ads in more magazines.

Before long, the business had expanded to take over our family room, dining room, living room, storage room, and kitchen. We bought a larger house, and moved the business into the basement. We rented mailing lists and sent direct mail advertising to hundreds of thousands of potential customers who didn't know and didn't care that we had no fancy offices or high-paid employees. Best of all, we never heard from the customers who didn't want our product, but only from those who did.

The business grew faster than we ever dreamed possible, but we still didn't hire full-time employees or move into an industrial park. We hired teenagers to help us fulfill orders, and we handled the bookkeeping ourselves. Our children got into the act as well, stuffing, stamping, and labeling when they came home from school. It was a happy and rewarding time in our lives.

Eventually, however, the business slowed down. Increases in the cost of postage reduced the profitability of direct mail advertising, and magazines began charging more for space ads. We were still selling as many books, but we weren't making as many profits. Market conditions had changed, and our business had to change accordingly. But because we had no overhead—no building lease, no business loans, no employees—it was easy to change. We simply let the business die out and moved into a more satisfying form of self-employment—a full-time investment writer for a publisher who, interestingly, had begun on a similar path, but took a different direction when he came to the fork in the road.

Our publisher, Tom Phillips, began his publishing business from his home as well, following the same conservative path I did of limiting costs and liabilities, reinvesting all profits, and testing markets before advertising heavily. As the business became too big for him to handle alone, he rented office space, hired some employees, and began to operate like a real business. Today, twenty years later, he owns an international company that employs over seven hundred people. But he still practices the principles of conservative growth and limited risk.

Keys to Business Success

These are the keys to starting a successful business:

- ♦ Examine your motives for going into business for yourself. Is it because you have a great idea for a product? Or is it because you're sick and tired of working nine to five for someone else? If it is the latter, I have news for you: you'll never have a harder boss to work for than yourself if you expect to be successful. Employees go home when their shifts are over; owners stay until the work is done or take the work home with them to worry about it there. Employees have a guaranteed paycheck, regardless of the profitability of the company; owners must pay the bills, employees, suppliers, collectors, landlords, and the like, regardless of whether the business is turning a profit.

I remember one time when we made a major advertising mistake. Riding high on previous successes, we used a new advertising campaign without testing it first. We sent a million pieces of direct mail advertising and bought a dozen ads in magazines before we realized that the ad would not bring in enough orders to make a profit. We had of course to fulfill the orders that did come in, even though there weren't enough to break even. Because of the volume of advertising, we worked night and day, knowing that the best we could hope for was to reduce our losses. Meanwhile, the people who worked for us continued to get paid as usual.

Still, despite the worries and risks, having a business of your own can be extremely rewarding, financially and psychologically. But you must follow through, even when you are exhausted. If you are the kind of person who knocks off early, calls in sick when the weather is nice, or spends money whenever it's in your pocket, starting a business will probably not work.

♦ Often the best source for your business is your current job. Many entrepreneurs discover the germ of a business from working in their current employment—a new, better way to do business.

♦ Begin with a product, not an office. Spend some time thinking about your talents and abilities. What can you produce that other people might need? More important, think about the needs of others. How can you convince potential customers that you can fulfill their needs for them? Many successful businesses start out as hobbies, and they target small audiences.

My brother, for example, loved photography from the time he was a young boy. His first job was as a clerk in a fast photo shop. His knowledge about photography was apparent, and he often gave free advice to customers about how to improve their photographs. Many of those customers asked my brother to take pictures for them, and he turned his hobby into a lucrative business, with a studio in his apartment. A couple of years later, the owner of the shop approached my brother with a business proposition: How would he like to buy the shop? My brother jumped at the chance. Now he could use the profits from the company to finance his real passion: taking photographs. He built a reputation as the best wedding photographer in the valley, and his clientele grew.

Then the business worries began to pile up on my brother. He found that he had less time for taking photographs, because he had to worry about suppliers, equipment repairs, bookkeeping, employees, and taxes. Eventually he sold the business and concentrated on what he does best: taking pictures.

♦ Start small. Don't jump into a full-time business of your own. You need time to test the markets, select suppliers, plan advertising, and hire employees. The wisest approach is to keep your present employment as a safety net while you begin a small business on the side. As the business becomes more and more successful, you will know the proper time to quit your job and take the plunge into full-time self-employment. Meanwhile, if the business never does become self-supporting, you can close it down and continue earning your paycheck, while you think about other business possibilities.

♦ Be aware that even the best ideas will fail if market conditions aren't right. That's why flexibility is so important. Our housekeeper is a good example of this. She is without doubt the best house cleaner in the country. She's smart, she's cheerful, she takes pride in her work. She sees things that need to be done without having to be told, and she is extremely reliable. A dream come true, in my opinion. A few years ago, recognizing that age would someday catch up with her, she decided to turn her skills into a full-time business that she could eventually direct from an office. Finding more clients wasn't a problem; with her reputation, she was soon cleaning thirty-five houses per week, with a staff of four employees who traveled together from house to house.

Meanwhile, Alice's husband was starting a business of his own, as a landscaper. Like Alice, Alan had a great reputation for being a smart, dedicated, reliable worker. He, too, built a large clientele and hired several workers. Together they were building quite a dynasty.

But there is a fundamental difference between yard work and housework. For some reason, people are willing to pay more for the former than for the latter. Alan could afford to pay his employees more than Alice could pay hers, and as a consequence, his employees were more reliable. Alice found herself competing for workers with the federal government, who would pay her labor pool almost as much to stay home collecting welfare as she could afford to pay them to clean houses. Moreover, Alice ran an honest business, paying employment taxes for all her employees. In essence, she was competing for clients with the underground economy, house cleaners who can afford to charge less per house because they are pocketing all of the money in cash.

You can probably guess what happened. Yes, Alice's business "failed." But the story has a happy ending. Alan's business continued to flourish. Because of his fine reputation, he landed some commercial contracts, and they no longer have to rely on Alice's business to make ends meet.

The point, of course, is to start small, build gradually, and be flexible. When you see a potential for making a profit, go after it. But if, after two years, you aren't making enough profit to take a day off once in a while, reconsider the business. If you are having trouble keeping employees, is it because the work is too hard, the pay too little, or the competition too stiff? If you aren't finding enough customers, is it because you aren't advertising effectively, your location is poor, or the product simply isn't in demand? Make adjustments, try again, give it your fullest effort for two years. But be willing to change your whole outlook if you aren't turning a profit after that time.

The New Revolution

You may not be aware of it, but there is a financial revolution going on: home-based businesses. It is how my wife and I started our business, and you may wish to consider it.

There are many reasons why home-based businesses have become successful. They are an easy, low-cost way to enter into the business marketplace. They are especially beneficial to mothers who want to be close to their young children. And they provide all the benefits of being in business as well as working from the comfort of your home.

In today's technologically sophisticated environment, you can run a business from home just as easily as from a storefront. With computers, faxes, cellular phones, modems, and video conferencing you can take your business to any location and operate.

Of course, I'm not talking about opening a grocery store or a car wash in your home, but there are hundreds of other lucrative business opportunities that you can run from your home.

All in the Family

One of the secrets of business is the value of the entire family. The family can play a key role in transforming a successful business into an enjoyable, profitable lifestyle. The family is, for example, a source of honest, dependable, and hard-working employees. The family can benefit in the following ways:

- ◆ The family business can be a perpetual asset, providing an income stream for generations.

- ◆ The family business is one of the best available tax shelters.

- ◆ The family business can provide an invaluable source of business and social experience for children.

- ◆ The family business can grow and be sold to finance a healthy and prosperous retirement.

- ◆ The family business can be a source of family unity and happiness.

- ◆ The family business, if properly devised, is one of the

few assets that you can pass on from one generation
to the next without being hit by estate taxes.

Put your family to work for you at an early age. This helps
them to develop respect for the business, to understand that small
businesses thrive on the care given to them by the owners. My
wife has a college student whose grandfather used to take him to
work every Saturday. The boy had his own desk and helped out in
his grandfather's work. They did this together every Saturday
from the time the boy was three years old until he was old enough
to do real work in the company. Today this young man is preparing to take over the family business.

Involving the family in the business early on will also allow you
to gauge their competence and fortitude. Business is not easy; it
takes hard work and persistence to succeed.

The Ultimate Tax Shelter

Owning your own business is the ultimate tax shelter. Instead of
an allowance, your children can get paid from business proceeds. As
long as it's under $1,400 per year, they are not liable for any income
taxes. They can also open their own Individual Retirement
Accounts, allowing them to earn even more money tax free, up to
$3,400 each. But, remember, they will be penalized for withdrawing
their money before they are fifty-nine and a half years old.

Your spouse, moreover, can work in a legitimate capacity for the
business. And the entire family can travel on legitimate company
business, free of personal taxes. The business in turn can write off a
good portion of the trip as an expense. But the key word here is
legitimate. The eyes of the IRS are on family businesses.

As a retirement planning tool, little can match a family business. You can set up a 401k plan for all your employees (including
family members) and have the company contribute to the plan.
Not only will your family tax bill shrink dramatically, your
investable income will increase as well.

Businesses of ten people or more get better rates on health insurance through various business associations and group discounts. The business can match or pay for its employees' (family members') health care on a pretax basis.

The company may also provide company cars for its employees as legitimate business expenses. Again, you can write off all costs associated with the business use of the vehicle, including insurance, maintenance, and car payments.

If your business is operated from your home, you can deduct the cost of utilities, insurance, property taxes, mortgage payments, and lawn care, as long as they are legitimate expenses associated with running the business from home.

If you do use home-office deductions, you should take the following precautions:

♦ Get a separate business phone set up for your office. Use it only for business purposes. If you advertise your business, use this number only and be sure to keep a record of the ads as proof of your intention.

♦ Make sure your listing appears in the business section of the phone book.

♦ If possible, have customers visit your home office on a regular basis, unless local zoning laws prevent such visits. Keep a log of these visits.

♦ Have your business mail sent to your home office address or a business post office box.

♦ Try to conduct as much business as possible in your home office.

♦ Be sure all business licenses issued by the state, county, and/or city reflect your home address.

♦ Beware of local laws limiting commercial activities at home.

Business Ideas—Where to Find Them

Is there a business that you've always wanted to have—a coffee shop, or a travel agency, or even a pet-sitting service? Whatever it is, you have to do some research before you get started.

What about a franchise?

If you are having trouble getting an idea, consider a franchise. Franchises are businesses that have already been developed, such as McDonald's and Jazzercise. All they require is capital and manpower to get going.

You can locate franchises through several sources. You can find them in major financial publications and business magazines to begin with, or at major exhibitions throughout the country. They are usually advertised in your local paper and held in large convention centers. Contact the convention center closest to you and ask for a schedule of events.

To get a list of some of the franchises offered, you can contact the International Franchise Association, or IFA. For $5 IFA will send you a Franchise Opportunity Guide with over five thousand franchises listed, information about franchising, legal technicalities, and a host of other information. It is well worth the cost. Call them at 800-543-1038 or 202-628-8000.

All That Glitters...
Perils and Pitfalls of Franchising

A college buddy of mine started his career as a night manager of a Ramada Inn. He lived frugally, saved much, and within a few years, he was offered an opportunity to buy a McDonald's franchise in southern California. Today he owns two McDonald's restaurants in Wyoming, and he's a millionaire in his mid-forties. The franchise business has been good to my old college buddy.

Another friend is part owner of a Subway franchise in Florida. He and his wife work fourteen hours a day, with one of them opening in the morning and the other one closing. The only time they see each other is at work, when their shifts overlap for the lunch rush. Yes, the business is turning a profit, but they have to split those profits with his silent partner who put up the funds to buy the franchise. He and his wife keep working at the business, and they are determined to make it a success. But sometimes it doesn't seem worth the trouble, especially when employees call in sick or quit without a day's notice. So far the franchise hasn't been the money maker he had hoped for.

These two stories illustrate the pro's and con's of the franchise business. Owning and operating a franchise can be a dream come true or a living nightmare.

How does it work? A franchise is a business that is based upon a successful marketing concept. This concept is duplicated in different locations under the ownership of different people. The franchiser, the company that sells you the concept, collects an initial fee and future royalties based on your sales. In return you receive the reputation, the bulk-buying services, the marketing, and the proven techniques that make the business run well.

The Good News

With franchises, the costs of research and time spent on developing an idea have been borne by someone else. You know what to expect. The marketing for the franchise is also already in place—the prices have been set, the suppliers contracted, and advertising campaigns scheduled. All you have to worry about is running the show. Because of the uniformity, customers know what to expect and you have an eager clientele waiting for you to open shop.

Franchises usually provide a powerful purchasing network. This leads to lower costs and higher margins for your business. Other advantages include assistance with legal, payroll, and benefits matters. Most important, though, franchises provide you with customers already familiar with your product.

The Bad News

To begin with, you generally need quite a bit of start-up capital. The franchise fee may cost as little as a few thousand dollars or as much as several hundred thousand. In addition, in order to participate fully, you must adhere strictly to the franchiser's specifications, which may include territory, the purchase or lease of buildings, and expensive equipment and inventory.

All franchises differ in quality and effectiveness. Some are better established, have better reputations, and provide better services and products. These qualities are not always apparent when consulting with a fast-talking franchise representative.

Perhaps the most unappealing aspect of franchises is the rules. This can be good for those who are scared of running the show, but it can stifle the creativity that makes self-employment fun. You have all the headaches of being in charge while still having to report to a boss.

Franchises are usually sold by territory in order to prevent competition between franchisees. But sometimes territories overlap. Worse still, you may end up with a location that is in the middle of nowhere or hampered by a difficult traffic pattern and lose rather than make money.

In order to limit your risk, follow some simple rules:

♦ Ask your local Better Business Bureau (BBB) if there are any complaints against the franchiser. Then call the BBB in the town where the franchiser is located.

♦ Contact your state Office of Consumer Affairs to discover if the franchiser is under investigation.

♦ If permitted, ask for audited payments of royalties and franchise fees from other franchises to the franchiser. This will indicate how well other stores within the chain are doing.

♦ Get a certified letter signed by the president of the franchise granting you an exclusive territory.

♦ To protect yourself from any undue pressure, insert a clause in the agreement providing for a mutually chosen third party to settle any disputes. Or at least make sure that the appeals process is not weighted heavily in favor of the franchiser. Hire your own attorney to review the contract carefully—relying on the franchiser's attorney to handle everything for you could prove to be a false economy.

♦ Check with other franchise owners to get their opinion. If possible, attend a convention of franchisees and listen carefully to the attendees as much as to the speakers.

What about Amway and Other Sales Organizations?

Many successful businesspeople have profited handsomely from Amway and other networking organizations. Amway continues to expand around the world because it offers a growing variety of products and financial services. Door-to-door selling has been replaced by people-to-people contacting. For entrepreneurs who are social extroverts and like direct selling, networking might be the right business. Others have found it unappealing. Networking works both ways. If you get a lot of people on your "downline," you can make a lot of money. If you are unable to find others to join you, your business will probably stagnate.

Sources of Information

Your local library has hundred of periodicals and books that are solely concerned with small businesses. The information is free. Magazines such as *Inc.* and *Entrepreneur* provide high-tech business ideas and sources.

One of the best sources for ideas and advice about business and home businesses in particular is CompuServe, mentioned earlier. This on-line service is a hotbed of ideas and information. Plug into one of the information forums and get almost any information you want from other active participants. They also have a specific section for home businesses.

Be wary, however, of going into business with someone you meet over the computer forum networks. These are strangers, no matter how friendly they seem, and you know nothing about them except what they tell you.

The Business Broker

Business brokers are another source of information on small businesses. They can provide you with listings of businesses that are for sale in your area. Business brokers get their fees from the seller, so be sure to use a reputable business broker. Contact your local business council or chamber of commerce.

Buying a business through a business broker is much like buying a house—there's a lot of negotiation. You should have a contingency clause that will let you out at the last minute without any penalty. And always ask for a clause that allows you to be on site at the business for a period of time, say three to four weeks. If the owner agrees, spend a month learning the business from the inside. If he disagrees, walk away.

Do Your Own Research

Many businesses are listed in the classified section of the newspaper. When pursuing these opportunities, it pays to do some groundwork. This can be less complicated and cheaper than using a business broker, but many of the same problems exist. Make sure that you are not getting taken.

The most common mistakes that buyers make concern numbers. Take my advice: Do not rely completely on the set of books presented by a business. Instead, obtain concrete proof of how a business is doing, say, through audited statements and filed tax returns from the last three years at least.

Your Automatic Investment Plan Will Help

If you should decide to go into business for yourself, one great source of investment capital will be your Automatic Investment Plan (AIP). You will be surprised to see how fast your investment account is growing. If you decide not to invest it in a business of your own, just relax and watch your investment account grow investing in other people's successful businesses, the stock market.

ACTIONS TO TAKE ON DAY 17

1. Consider the high rewards awaiting you by starting your own business.
2. Do the research necessary to select the right business for you—minimize your risk of failure!
3. Don't forget to keep adding to your AIP. It will provide the seed capital to start a new business.

BIG MONEY ON LITTLE
REAL ESTATE DEALS

Today we are going to discuss a great way to make money on the side—real estate. Despite what you may have heard, income-producing properties are still a great source of profits. Many people are becoming financially independent through real estate.

The Power of Leverage

In 1987 one of my students asked me for advice on buying a house. He had just completed his MBA and landed a good job. He found a house in an up-and-coming neighborhood that was on the market for $99,000, reduced from $119,000. The owner had lived there for thirty-eight years and owned the home free and clear.

The only problem was that the student could only afford $85,000. I told him to go ahead and make an offer.

The first rule for buying real estate or any negotiable item is to make an offer. Never take the asking price as final. There is always a built-in cushion for negotiation. If you don't use it, you will always pay too much. My student said he felt stupid offering such a low price for such a nice house. Besides, he would have to offer less than the $85,000 in order to have room for negotiating. My advice to him was to go ahead. The worst thing that could happen was that the offer would be rejected. Big deal! Since the owner held the mortgage free and clear, I also advised trying to obtain owner financing. The second rule for buying real estate is never assume that the seller will reject your offer. You don't know what the seller's position is. Maybe he needs the money quickly, or is in the middle of a divorce, or hasn't received any offers on the property and is desperate for the first one. You'll never know until you make the offer.

The offer was made. It consisted of a $75,000 purchase price, $24,000 less than the asking price and $44,000 less than the original price, with owner financing over thirty years at 8 percent. (Interest rates for homes were running at 10 percent at that time.) The homeowner countered with $80,000, over fifteen years at 8.5 percent. The deal was done!

The owner financing was a big plus. It reduced closing costs by over $3,000. There were no points involved, and the owner paid over $1,300 to tent the house for termites. The owner financing also allowed them to complete the transaction in a matter of weeks. No finance companies were involved, no long credit reports, and no anguished waiting for a reply from the bank.

After putting $10,000 down, their monthly payment on the $75,000 balance was $689 for fifteen years. The thirty-year mortgage would have been about $125 less each month. The higher payment seemed like a hard decision at the time, but today they are already halfway through the payments and were recently offered the opportunity to pay off the rest of the mortgage, about $45,000, at a discount.

And that's not even the half of it. Their house appreciated over 150 percent during the next seven years. It is now worth more than $200,000. That is the beauty of owning a single-family home. For their initial $10,000 investment, plus payments of just under $60,000 to date, they could walk away from the deal richer by $85,000. That represents a 750 percent return on their investment without even figuring in the tax benefits and the rent they would have had to pay if they hadn't owned the house. If you consider the rent as well, then their return on the original $10,000 has returned 1,300 percent over seven years.

Obviously they were very lucky to buy a house in an area where property values exploded. But, even if their house had appreciated by only 5 percent every year, they would still have received a very positive return on their original $10,000 investment. At 5 percent a year, the house would be worth about $113,000 today. Therefore, they would have earned over $33,000 on their initial investment, over 200 percent, almost 20 percent annually—before figuring the tax advantages.

This is the power of real estate when leverage is used wisely. In my opinion, your home is one of the safest investments you can make if you buy at the right price. Not only will you enjoy the benefits of home ownership, you could also receive a potentially high return on your money.

Real Estate Bargains in the 1990s

The fallout from this past recession and the Savings and Loan crisis of the eighties can provide you with endless opportunities for bargain housing, both for personal residence and investments. Buying bargain real estate takes a little more time and groundwork than just calling up a broker and asking for current listings. But it is possible if you follow my plan. Try it and see.

Foreclosures

Let me give another example of how profitable real estate can be, especially in today's foreclosures. Another one of my students is a retired investor interested in income-producing properties, but he had never purchased a foreclosed property before. One day he got a call from his real estate broker, who suggested that he attend a distressed property auction held by the Veterans Administration (VA). Together they looked through the offerings in his hometown in northern Florida. They found a low-priced, three-bedroom, two-bath house that had recently been foreclosed. It was appraised for $60,000. They checked the house out. Everything looked fine, so they decided to bid on the property. Naturally, there were many other bargain hunters bidding on the house, since real estate promoters have pushed the idea that buying foreclosures is an easy way to make money. Despite substantial competition, my student got the property for only $41,000, even though his bid was lower than some of the others.

Why? Because he offered to pay *cash* for the house! The VA as well as other government agencies favor cash bids over financing. Cash is king. The cash-poor investor is in a weak bargaining position when the cash-rich investor comes along. (And if you are adding regularly to your Automatic Investment Plan, you'll have the money to make an all-cash offer!)

My student rented the house for $425 a month. He took out a $30,000 mortgage, which gives him over $100 a month positive cash flow. When he sells the house, he will make a huge profit.

Where to Look for Foreclosures

Now is a good time to hunt for bargains because of the especially large inventory of foreclosed properties being offered by banks and government agencies.

The best place to look for most distress sales is in the public and legal notices section in local newspapers. Contact the local county or city official to find out which newspapers carry these notices. Investing in foreclosed properties is a popular business, and many investors attend those sales regularly. You must do your homework before others beat you to it.

Another excellent source for foreclosed properties is the Resolution Trust Corporation, which has thousands of properties in its inventory. A custom report created by state, county, or zip code is available free of charge. To order call 800-782-3006.

Other government agencies also sell foreclosed properties. They are the Federal National Mortgage Association (Fannie Mae), the U.S. Department of Housing and Urban Development (HUD), and the VA.

Get a current list of foreclosures by state or county from Fannie Mae by contacting them at Foreclosures, 1 North Charles Street, Suite 1503, Baltimore, Maryland 21201.

HUD and the VA can be contacted locally. Check the government listings in your phone book for the number of your nearest office. Often these properties are advertised in your local real estate section and listed with local agents.

Looking for Distress

When searching for foreclosed properties or any real estate "deal" be sure you have your priorities and game plan lined up. Just because a property may be available for a very low price does not mean it is a good deal. You should set your sights on properties that are in distress due to the owner's inability to pay, not because they have been abandoned due to their location or condition. You are looking for a bargain, not a money pit. Remember the following rules before buying a foreclosed property:

♦ Be sure to get a look at the inside of the property with a certified home inspector. If this is not possible, check the architectural plans on file at the local courthouse. At least you will get a look at the floor plan. The courthouse should also have filings for any improvements that required a permit and, more important, a record of any deficiencies that might have been filed against the home-owners.

♦ Check with local real estate agents for prices of comparable homes that have recently sold in the neighborhood. This information is also available at the county or city tax department.

♦ Know how much you can afford to pay and how much you are willing to add in improvements before you enter the auction process. No need to grab the first opportunity. There are many more where this came from.

♦ Don't pursue a house only because it is low priced. As mentioned earlier, the object is to get a good deal in a good area, not a good deal in a bad area.

♦ Be sure to get a clean title. This can be done through a title search, which may cost a couple of hundred dollars. One may have already been conducted by the lender. Check first. If the house does not have a clear title, find out what the liens are. Many people immediately reject any house that has liens attached. This may thin the opposition.

The Fix-up Method

Probably the best deal you can find is a house that needs renovations. The fix-up approach made Bill Nickerson's book, *How I Turned $1,000 into $1,000,000 in Real Estate—In My Spare Time*, into a bestseller. Today he's up to $3 million.

Most people are too scared to deal with a house that needs to be rehabbed. But keep in mind that this opportunity has meant fortunes for some people who could look around and see what houses in good condition in the same neighborhood were selling for. A "rehab" house may sell far below market value, but it may in fact need only cosmetic improvement to get it back into shape. Hire a contractor or architect for a couple of hours to walk through the house and give you an idea of what it would cost to renovate. You may be surprised. The cost may not be so high, especially if you do some of the labor like painting and wall-papering yourself.

Just remember, look only for bad houses in good neighborhoods, not good houses in bad neighborhoods.

Your Automatic Investment Plan, Again

Where will you get the money for a down payment on an income-producing property? Where else but your Automatic Investment Plan (AIP)! Remember, this is ready money you can use instantly for a down payment.

Bargains come along every once in a while in real estate. Take advantage of them with your investments, and you'll be on the road to financial independence in no time.

ACTIONS TO TAKE ON DAY 18

1. Real estate can be a hidden treasure—start today to look for undervalued properties.
2. Invest in foreclosed or "rehab" properties in good neighborhoods.
3. Build your AIP to fund your real estate investments.

DAY
19

MAKE "LADY LUCK" WORK FOR YOU

Several years ago, I was flying TWA on my way to New York. I got on the airline and settled down in my seat. The stewardess offered me a drink and then, unexpectedly, a little card. At the time, TWA and the other airlines were offering "scratch off" cards to customers. The card had three boxes. I was told to scratch off each box and if there was an airplane image in all three boxes, I would win a prize—a free trip anywhere TWA flies. It didn't cost me anything to participate, so I took the card and scratched off the boxes.

I was the only one on the airline to win.

My free trip was to Italy and Israel—one of my most enjoyable vacations.

During our lifetimes, the ephemeral gods occasionally bless us with a lucky prize. Life is full of lucky opportunities, but the point of this story is that you must place yourself in a position to be lucky.

That's what Day 19 is all about.

Today is not, however, about how to win a sweepstakes or the lottery. The chances of hitting the jackpot are too small for my tastes, even though I've been an occasional winner. Today I'm going to describe some of the most challenging and aggressive ways to achieve financial independence. Mind you, this is not for everyone, and I by no means want to suggest that it can take the place of our basic strategy of diversified, automatic investing—the Automatic Investment Plan (AIP). Still, you might want to learn some of the basic techniques of investing if you should ever come across an outstanding opportunity that could make 1,000 percent on your money.

Am I joking? Not at all. Examples: If you invested $1,000 in McDonald's stock in 1971, you'd have $41,000 today, not counting dividends. If you invested $1,000 in GEICO stock, it is now worth $119,000. And $1,000 invested in Telefonos de Mexico, the giant Mexican telephone company, is worth almost $125,000. There are literally hundreds of examples of once small companies that have multiplied over and over again and made thousands of shareholders rich. They include Microsoft, Taco Bell, Blockbuster, Toys R Us, Coca Cola, and Wal-Mart.

What's the secret? Hitch yourself to a company with spectacular growth and over the long run you will get rich. As J. Paul Getty once said, "Buy into companies and industries that cannot help but burgeon as time goes by."

I have already introduced to you some basic investment ideas through mutual funds and automatic investing, and this remains a very safe and sure way to financial security. But how about investing in individual companies, many of which have the potential of skyrocketing in value if you get in on the ground floor? That's what this day's information is all about. If you put yourself in a position to profit from these growing junior companies, you have "lady luck" on your side. How then do you do it?

You don't need to pray for a lucky lotto ticket or an inheritance from a long lost uncle to make you rich. If you know what to do and how to do it, investing in the stock markets can make your fortune while you sleep. And the odds are much better than playing the lotto. At least when you buy a share of stock you will most likely have some value left after the Saturday night drawing. And if history is any type of guide, your holding will appreciate significantly over time.

But beware: Most investors buy at the top because they don't have the right sources or the right advice. In order to join the few who do get into these companies before the rest of the crowd, you must have insight and a good source of information. This does not mean that you should seek insider information or buy investments based on rumor. It means that you must develop a network of contacts and information sources that will do the work for you and bring you the ideas before the mainstream even begins to smell the coffee. Here are three ways to successful investing.

Your Inside Source to Big Money

One of the best aids is a financial newsletter that specializes in discovering new or emerging companies that have the potential of a Microsoft or McDonald's. Don't subscribe to any investment digest that merely recycles old information. You need advisors who visit these companies before anyone else, write about them before they become headlines, and recommend them before they are featured on financial talk shows.

Your investment advisor must also be able to perform. The companies that are recommended must have a strong potential for growth and price appreciation. People must want to buy the product. I remember a company that was on the cutting edge of home cholesterol testing. The subject was in vogue, and the company had been working on the technology for ten years. Unfortunately, a competitor beat it in introducing a home-test product. The result: the company's shares nosedived, and the competitor's share price skyrocketed. The advisor who recommended the first company was right about the technology, but he forgot to check the neighborhood.

Most publishing companies will be glad to send you complimentary copies of their newsletters, and some will also send you performance records. This is just the first step.

Next you must choose from among the dozens of newsletters until you find one that you are comfortable with. Is it easy to understand? Can you follow the recommendations? Does the editor's argument make sense? Are you interested in global investments and emerging markets? If so, make sure the advisor actually travels to these places or has correspondent offices overseas. Are you looking for growth? If so, it makes little sense to subscribe to a retirement newsletter that recommends income-oriented investments.

Once you have subscribed, you should track the investments on paper for six months to a year. Did the newsletter provide the returns it promised? Were the assumptions, insights, and information correct or were they just guesses?

I recommend subscribing to several newsletters at once, so you get a sense of dialogue going among advisors. Whenever I meet a subscriber who says, "I canceled all my other newsletters and only read yours, Mr. Skousen," it makes me shudder. You need to hear a variety of voices. Read over a dozen newsletters regularly.

Recommended Newsletters

Here are a few I recommend:

♦ *Charles Allmon's Growth Stock Advisory*, 4405 East-West Highway, Suite 305, Bethesda, Maryland 20814. Allmon specializes in the fastest growing companies in the United States and has an excellent track record. For several years, he has been bearish on the stock market in general and has maintained a large cash position in his portfolio, but if you concentrate on his small list of recommended stocks, you'll be a wealthy person in short order.

♦ *Taipan*, published by Agora Publishing, Inc., 826 E. Baltimore Street, Baltimore, Maryland 21202. The financial editor is Karim Rahemtulla, one of the researchers for this book. Karim invests regularly in new companies with rapid growth potential—before the price goes through the roof. From time to time, he mentions his prospects in *Taipan*.

For example, in July 1992 he recommended Silicon Graphics (NYSE: SGI) at $8.75 after seeing the company's advanced graphics at a trade show and investigating the company. In early 1994, it was selling for $26⅞, after the media had discovered the company.

♦ From time to time, my newsletter, *Forecasts & Strategies*, also recommends growth companies with outstanding prospects. Here's one of my best examples: in the early nineties, I discovered a Canadian-based company called International Retail Systems Inc. (Toronto: IRE), which provides state-of-the-art software for cash registers and point-of-sales systems at gas stations, department stores, and specialty shops. The price was around $1. After concluding agreements with NCR, Amoco, Arco, and Kmart, the stock took off and rose to $4.

Do Your Own Homework

The best way to make lady luck work for you is to do some groundwork yourself. Ask your friends, family, and coworkers if they know of any good companies that they deal with or have heard of. Do some research and some footwork. If the company is local, pay it a visit.

This is the technique Peter Lynch, former manager of the Magellan Fund, calls the "power of common knowledge." He initially hears about good companies through his family and friends. Examples include Taco Bell, Hanes, and Toys R Us.

By showing interest in the company before it is known, you have developed an inside track. The management is usually hungry for potential investors in the early years and will be more than willing to please you.

A good source of up and coming companies—one that is often maligned—is the NASDAQ Market and the Pink Sheets or OTC Bulletin Boards. Many of the companies listed on these exchanges are young emerging growth companies. Microsoft and Intel were once small NASDAQ stocks. Now they are both billion dollar companies still listed on the NASDAQ Exchange.

But do thorough research into these companies. Many fail for lack of capital, bad management decisions, or competition. Moreover, fraud is sometimes evident within the penny stock crowd. Penny stocks offer tremendous potential, but they are pretty risky.

Ask for a 10K

Ask the company to send you a 10K, a mandatory annual disclosure document that the company must file with the Securities and Exchange Commission. This document should provide all the information you need at a quick glance. If you become more interested, ask for more information, such as brochures and phone numbers and addresses of people who are familiar with their product or service.

When you are satisfied that the company is legitimate, with the potential to grow, invest some money, but only some. The whole point of this exercise is to invest a little bit into a promising company that might turn into a whole lot for the future. You may wish to use some of your AIP funds to invest in these "fast growth" companies, but don't overdo it.

Risk

Risk is the most important component of investing. A high risk speculative issue like penny stocks may be fine for people in their thirties or forties, but for someone close to retirement, it is unwise because the losses generally cannot be recouped easily.

If you are not comfortable with the risk of investing in small growth companies, you may wish to stick with no-load mutual funds that specialize in aggressive growth stocks. Some of the funds recommended on Day 4 fit into this category. Here are several other aggressive growth funds with a good track record:

♦ 20th Century Ultra Fund, 800-345-2021

♦ Evergreen Limited Market Fund, 800-235-0064

♦ Janus Venture Fund, 800-525-8983

♦ Mutual Series—Discovery Fund, 800-553-3014

The D Word, Again

Discipline always seems to rear its head when it comes to finance and investing. Once you decide upon a program, you must stick to it. If you keep changing your focus, or relying on short-term investing, you will never get ahead. One of the greatest modern-day market geniuses, Warren Buffett, is the master of simplicity in investing. And it has paid off handsomely by any account. Buffett's holdings are now worth more than the profits of companies like AT&T and Intel combined! His secret? Buy a few good companies (Coca Cola, GEICO, Capital Cities/ABC) and hold them for the long term.

Develop strong discipline. If you say you are going to invest $250 per month into Schwab's AIP, make sure you have that much money in the bank at all times.

Lower the Cost of Your Investment

If you are excited by investing in individual stocks, you have to have a broker. Many people throw away hard-earned money on full service brokers, paying 300 or 400 percent more in commission than discount brokers would charge to buy the same shares. Every hundred dollars you pay a broker is a hundred dollars less you have to earn money for you.

Full-service brokers charge as much as 5 percent of the total dollar amount of the trade in commissions, which can cut deeply into your profits. Discount brokers, on the other hand, charge between 0.5 and 1 percent, depending on dollar or share volume of the trade and the broker that is used. Some brokers trade stocks at a flat rate, $30, no matter how much stock you buy or sell.

Many large discount brokerage firms have regional offices. Selecting a discount broker should involve more than just a cost comparison. The broker's location is important. If you have a problem, you may wish to go directly to his office rather than risk being put on hold or getting a busy signal. During the crash of 1987, some brokers were too frightened to talk to their customers, who subsequently suffered larger losses.

Before you open an account, ask a representative to walk you through the monthly statements. Have him or her explain the following:

- number of shares bought/sold in a transaction
- commission schedule and handling charges
- cash or securities balances as marked on the statement
- interest rate and balance information if margin is used
- customer service telephone number
- interest amount paid you on credit balances

Which Discount Broker Should You Use?

There are quite a few discount brokers to choose from: Charles Schwab, Jack White, Fidelity, Quick & Reilly, Kennedy Cabot, and many more. Probably your best bet is to use the brokerage firm that handles your AIP. If you have a Schwab AIP, use Schwab to buy individual stocks. You can use your brokerage account that handles your AIP. It's that simple.

A Rich Man's Pearl of Wisdom

Let me end this day's activities with a fable. A young man was planning a long journey across the desert. Before he left, a wise old man came to him and said, "Half-way through your journey, you will come to an oasis where you will find some rocks lying on the ground. Pick up some of these rocks and put them into your pocket. At the end of the journey, you will be both happy and sad. Promise me you will do this."

The young man didn't quite understand, but out of respect, he decided to take the old man's advice. The trip was long and hard. Finally he arrived at the oasis. He was tired, but at the last minute, he picked up a few of the rocks and tossed them into his pockets before continuing his journey. When he arrived at his destination, he unpacked his bags and rested from his long journey. Suddenly he remembered the rocks. He reached into his pocket and, to his great surprise and delight, he discovered that those ordinary rocks had turned into valuable rubies.

As he reflected upon the wise man's promise, he realized that he truly was both happy and sad. Happy, because he now had rubies; sad, because he hadn't picked up more rocks when he could.

This parable applies to the world of investing, especially in growth stocks. When you make money, you're both happy and sad—happy that you made the money, but sad that you didn't invest more!

Investing can often be frustrating. You must take a long-term view, and not be concerned about making the "big killing." Steady progress can be achieved by investing in growth stocks and mutual funds that invest in growth companies.

Always be on the lookout for rocks that can turn into rubies.

ACTIONS TO TAKE ON DAY 19

1. Make a pledge not to get involved in lotteries and other gambling methods.

2. Make "lady luck" work for you by searching for new companies that have the potential to make it big.

3. Subscribe to newsletters and other services that specialize in fast-growing public companies.

4. Use a small part of your investment account to speculate in potential super growth companies.

OPEN YOUR EYES TO
THE NEW FRONTIER

Today we are going to broaden our vision even further, beyond those incredible opportunities in the United States, and focus instead on the wide world of investing.

Today I want you to consider investing some of your surplus funds in the stock markets of the world. On Day 4, we already discussed briefly the benefits of investing in global "emerging markets." In this chapter, I explain why this is such an exciting area of investment and why your wealth will increase more dramatically if you invest outside the United States.

Limiting yourself to investing in the North American markets is a mistake. Doing so will eliminate 70 percent of your opportunities for investment.

Thirty years ago the United States was the major player in the world equity markets, with about 68 percent of the market. All foreign markets, including Japan and Europe, made up only 32 percent of the total capitalization of world stocks. Today the tables are turned, and although the United States is still the biggest cook in the kitchen, its role has been diminished considerably. This means that you are literally missing the investment boat by avoiding international investing.

Some money managers disagree. Warren Buffett, the Omaha billionaire whose Berkshire Hathaway fund has risen from $500 a share to $20,000 today, argues that if investors can't find opportunities in America's $4 trillion market, they should stay out of the investment business.

There are plenty of opportunities in the United States, but why ignore the incredible global marketplace? America has a vibrant economy, but its growth rate pales in comparison to some of the emerging and reemerging markets of the world. Moreover, most of the top U.S. companies are international in scope, including one of Warren Buffett's favorite companies, Coca Cola. If Coca Cola, IBM, and Ford are going international, shouldn't you?

There is nothing un-American about investing globally, trading with companies that, in turn, trade with us. We all gain by international trade.

Incredible Growth Around the World

As an investment writer and economist, I've traveled to over fifty countries and lived in six. The world is an exciting place and new opportunities abound.

Free markets are expanding everywhere—in India, China, Chile, and the Czech Republic. Formerly communist countries and "third world" nations are trying to catch up with the rest of the world. Their leaders know that they must grow rapidly in order to develop into first world nations.

With the demise of the Soviet Union, many countries that relied on the Soviets for much of their foreign trade must now open their doors to the world. India, for example, has had to lift trade restrictions, lower tariffs, promote infrastructure development, and reduce taxes on its investment community in order to survive. As a result, it has prospered as never before.

Other nations have also rejected socialism and central planning and are growing accordingly. The supply-side revolution is gaining ground everywhere.

The Second Mexican Revolution

Take Mexico, for example. For years, our friend to the south was known for its inflation, corruption, government waste, poverty, and foreign debt. As a result, Mexico had a constant exodus of people and capital. Then Carlos Salinas, a Harvard-trained economist, was elected in 1988. He took bold steps to turn his country around. He refinanced Mexico's $100 billion debt, while at the same time sharply curtailing monetary growth and reducing inflation from 200 percent to 10 percent a year. His government began a massive privatization campaign to get rid of overbloated nationalized industries, including Telefonos de Mexico. Salinas reformed Mexico's state-run oil monopoly and cleaned up the corrupt labor unions. He cut marginal income tax rates and eliminated—eliminated!—the capital gains tax. His party announced sweeping economic reforms that allowed foreign investors to have majority ownership of Mexican-based enterprises. His government helped push through the North American Free Trade Agreement, the free-trade agreement among the United States, Canada, and Mexico.

As a result of these free market measures, Mexico grew as never before, and capital flowed back into Mexico by the billions. The Mexican bolsa skyrocketed. And, for the first time in decades, Mexico had a surplus in its federal budget last year!

This is not to say Mexico has done everything right. They still face a lot of problems. For example, pegging the peso to the dollar created a major crisis for the new Zedillo regime in 1994-95.

Chile and Argentina: Other Models of Reform

In many ways, Salinas learned his economic lessons from Chile. Under military strongman Augusto Pinochet, Chile overthrew the Marxist regime and adopted the menu of the Chicago Boys, a group of free enterprise economists, for economic success: free trade, tax cuts, privatization, and control of the money supply. The Chileans call it "The Quiet Revolution." Chile went through a series of crises in the mid-1970s and early 1980s, but it is now growing faster than any other country in Latin America. Under the system of a true free market, the entire country is booming— from the south, which raises fruits and vegetables, to the north, famous for its mining. Chile even privatized its social security system! Representatives of many third world nations have come to learn how the Chilean model works. It has been so successful that Pinochet's successor, Patricio Aylwin, a "socialist," has endorsed the free market reforms.

Adopting the methods of the economic miracles of Chile and Mexico, Carlos Menem has made a dramatic difference in Argentina. Argentina used to be the wealthiest nation in Latin America, but decades of national socialism, runaway inflation, and protectionism under the Peronistas reduced it to third world status. Menem, the leader of the Peronista party, surprised everyone by reversing course, cutting taxes, lowering trade barriers, privatizing, and deregulating the economy. In short, Argentina is back on the road to recovery.

Lessons from the Asian Economic Miracles

The world's fastest growing region is Asia, especially Southeast Asia. Supergrowth is evident everywhere. The leaders in China,

Hong Kong, South Korea, Taiwan, Malaysia, Thailand, Indonesia, and now even Vietnam, all know the formula: supply-side, free market economics! The government leaders have institutionalized pro-growth policies—free trade, little or no taxes on savings and investments, capital formation and public infrastructure, fiscal and monetary restraint, avoidance of a large welfare state, and strong emphasis on higher education and training. They reject the Keynesian policy of promoting consumption at the expense of saving. That's what I call enlightened industrial policy!

Japan utilized many of these supply-side policies to achieve its own economic miracle following World War II. Much of the leadership was provided by Americans—General Douglas MacArthur, economist Carl Shoup, banker Joseph Dodge, and quality-control engineer Edwards Deming.

The Crisis in Japan

Japan used to be at the head of the pack, but has been drawn into its own mire primarily because its leaders adopted Western-style economics in the late 1980s. The Bank of Japan artificially lowered interest rates and expanded the money supply rapidly in the mid-1980s, creating a superboom in stocks, real estate, and the economy. Then in the late 1980s, it recognized that it had gone too far and abruptly switched to a tight-money policy. At the same time, Tokyo, under pressure from Washington, raised taxes and imposed a capital gains tax for the first time. As a result, the Japanese stock and real estate markets collapsed and the economy floundered. It has only recently made a slow recovery, but it is not likely to return to its glory until the Japanese elect a prime minister who understands sound supply-side economics and has the ability to lead.

The New Indian Guru: Free-Market Competition!

For decades, economists and investors had written off India as a basket case. John Templeton, the mutual fund magnate, tells the story of when he took a world tour in the 1930s. He visited India and saw the poverty, and he visited Hong Kong and saw the poverty. Fifty years later, he took the same world tour. He visited India and saw the poverty, and then visited Hong Kong and saw the... wealth! What made the difference? Government leadership! Templeton concluded: "The Indian government regulates nearly everything, so there's very little progress; whereas in Hong Kong the government keeps its hands off."

Today change is taking place in India, too. Gandhi's anti-capitalist mentality, his opposition to machinery and foreign capital, has been discredited. Long live the free market! Sociologists used to say that the Indian people were culturally different from the Chinese and the Westerners, that their Hindu economics was fundamentally opposed to the "materialistic" god of capitalism. Now we see the truth. Once government got off the backs of the people, we discovered that the Indians are no different from anyone else. They want to enjoy a higher standard of living for themselves and their families. They, too, are entrepreneurs.

Change for India's 900 million people, the world's largest democracy, began in 1991, when Narasimha Rao came to power. Prior to this time, India had a centrally planned bureaucratic nightmare, in some ways worse than the former Soviet Union's. New Delhi imposed high taxes, issued licenses, and protected local businesses from foreign competition. As a result, India never grew much.

Now India is rapidly changing from a command economy to a market economy. Tariffs have been cut in half and will be cut even further. Marginal tax rates have been reduced. Nationalized industries are being privatized. Much more needs to be done, including full convertibility of the rupee and a much-needed public infrastructure, but the direction is clear—more economic freedom. No longer do businessmen have to get permission from New Delhi to carry on their business.

The result: India is growing like never before. In 1993 its Gross Domestic Product was up 4.5 percent. The trade deficit declined from $2.6 billion in 1992 to $440 million in 1993. Inflation has declined steadily to under 10 percent. Interest rates dropped from 20 percent to 14 percent. And the India stock market has risen spectacularly.

This all came about because a new leader was elected and took the initiative to make changes for the better.

The Italian Connection

Changes are taking place in Europe as well. In Italy, an amazing thing happened on the way to the forum: Rome has made a dramatic turnabout. Fed up with inflation, taxes, bureaucracy, and labor power, the Italians booted out the establishment and replaced it with a new government with tremendous potential. Can you believe that 80 percent of the new electorate to the National Assembly has never held office before? Nor had Italy's charismatic new prime minister, multimillionaire business tycoon Silvio Berlusconi. This is Italy's fifty-fourth change in power since World War II, but it could be the first radical departure from the past.

Berlusconi's party, Forza Italia, favors lower taxes, investment incentives, liberalized labor laws, and further privatization. Supply-side economics may have been recently out of fashion in the United States, but not in Italy.

Spain: The Fiesta's Over

Not every country has the right kind of leaders. Some nations have still to learn the principles of sound economics and prosperity. Many continue to suffer from the wrong kind of leadership.

Spain is a tragic example of bad leadership. Just a decade ago, Spain was Europe's great hope. After the demise of the Franco regime in 1975, the country advanced quickly. Foreign companies rushed to tap its market of 39 million citizens. Europeans flocked to its resorts on the Mediterranean. Spain joined the European Community.

Then everything went sour. Today Spain's unemployment rate is at depression levels, 25 percent, the highest in the world. Gillette, Colgate-Palmolive, Suzuki Motors, and other multi-national corporations are leaving. The nation is at a standstill.

Who's to blame? The man at the top—Prime Minister Felipe Gonzalez, the charismatic socialist leader who has headed the government for twelve years. During his administration, the government embraced a massive social agenda, including free health care and heavily subsidized university education. As a result, deficits grew and inflation rose. Businesses were required to give workers life-time employment contracts, while the state offered generous unemployment benefits. As result, many big businesses stopped hiring. If you can't fire anyone, why hire?

When the recession hit Spain in 1991, the country fell apart and the overbloated government was exposed. Now more than ever, Spain needs new leadership to heal the wounded and get the country back on its feet.

Venezuela: A Tragic Example

Venezuela is another example of poor leadership. For decades, Venezuela has suffered from politicians who took advantage of the country's large oil reserves. Oil made Venezuela the richest country in Latin America, but, tragically, its leaders could not live within their budgets and inflation exploded in the 1980s. Recently the country brought back a former president, Rafael Caldera, who has wrecked havoc on the nation, imposing draconian price and exchange controls and eliminating civil liberties. Needless to say, Venezuela is suffering from a major depression—in the midst of prosperity in the rest of South America.

How to Profit: Country Funds

Clearly the way to profit from the incredible changes taking place in the world is to invest in countries that have adopted sound economics and avoid investing in those nations that maintain a high degree of socialism.

The best way to invest globally is to buy into "country funds," mutual funds that specialize in a specific nation's stock market. They usually trade on the New York Stock Exchange. Examples include:

- ◆ Chile Fund (NYSE: CH)
- ◆ China Fund (NYSE: CHN)
- ◆ Emerging Markets Telecommunications Fund (NYSE: ETF)
- ◆ GT Greater Europe Fund (NYSE: GTF)
- ◆ India Growth Fund (NYSE: IGF)
- ◆ Italy Fund (NYSE: ITF)
- ◆ Japan OTC Equities Fund (NYSE: JOF)
- ◆ Korea Equity Fund (NYSE: KEF)
- ◆ Latin America Fund (NYSE: LAF)
- ◆ Malaysia Fund (NYSE: MF)
- ◆ Mexico Fund (NYSE: MXF)
- ◆ Morgan Stanley Emerging Markets Fund (NYSE: MSF)
- ◆ Scudder New Asia Fund (NYSE: SAF)
- ◆ Scudder New Europe Fund (NYSE: NEF)
- ◆ Singapore Fund (NYSE: SGF)
- ◆ Taiwan Fund (NYSE: TWF)
- ◆ Templeton Emerging Markets Fund (NYSE: EMF)

You can buy any of the above funds through your discount broker. In addition, there are a variety of no-load "emerging market" mutual funds to choose from, including Lexington Emerging Markets Fund, Montgomery Global Telecommunications Fund, and GT Global Emerging Markets Fund. You can purchase these funds directly from the fund family or through a discount broker.

Buying Individual Foreign Stocks

You can also buy individual foreign stocks. Hundreds of foreign stocks trade on the New York Stock Exchange or NASDAQ as American depository receipts (ADRs). Ask your broker for a list. Then do your homework by studying the outlook for these companies. Check your local library for information from *Value Line Investment Survey* or *Standard and Poor's Stock Guide*.

You may also wish to buy foreign stocks directly on foreign exchanges (London, Zurich, Tokyo, Hong Kong, Sidney, etc.). Many brokers specialize in this area. From time to time, I recommend individual foreign issues and a specific broker to buy from in my newsletter, Forecasts & Strategies (800-777-5005). But, bear in mind that buying these foreign issues involves a greater degree of risk. Moreover, they are not usually quoted in the *Wall Street Journal*, so you don't know their value each day unless you call your broker.

One More Time: CompuServe

For updated information on foreign stocks (as well as U.S. stocks), check out CompuServe. Not only can you get fifteen-minute delayed quotes on stocks that trade in the United States, but also a host of other important information that will help you to follow your foreign investments closely.

The historical quote section of CompuServe will allow you to pull up quotes on ADRs that trade on the bulletin boards. You can also retrieve news stories and company information such as insider selling, financial statements, and management information.

In addition, the databases help you create charts and pull up historical information. Current financial news from almost every financial center in the world is available along with intelligence bulletins for each country. This information can be found in the Company Information section under the Citibank Global Report section. Dividend, split, warrant, and option information is also available in the Company Information section. A host of other information ranges from articles in business periodicals, magazines, and industry newsletters to currency quotes and commodities prices.

The only catch is the expense of using the system. Although not nearly so expensive as professional services like Reuters or Bloomberg, intensively using CompuServe (which I recommend over every other on-line service such as Prodigy or America Online) could cost you between $25 and $100 depending on the information you want.

Investing in foreign shares is no longer as speculative as it once was. With today's better reporting and information systems, you can improve your investment potential by including foreign markets in your portfolio. These countries represent superior growth and income potential. Don't discount your profits by limiting yourself to local markets.

ACTIONS TO TAKE ON DAY 20

1. Consider investing in foreign countries offering higher economic growth rates and emerging market potential.

2. Check out country funds and no-load emerging market funds through your discount broker.

3. If you are willing to take higher risks, examine the high profit potential of individual foreign stocks by investing directly on foreign exchanges through a U.S. broker.

REVIEW AND MEDITATION

This week we have tried to expand your horizons quite literally by taking you completely around the world in your quest for financial independence. Today, as you review and meditate, think about the various assets you possess. Not your financial assets; we'll do that tomorrow, with "Financial Checkup II." For today, think about your intangible assets. How can you put them to better use so that you can stop worrying about job security and start enjoying life more abundantly?

Count Your Blessings by Listing Your Assets

For some people, a new job or a business of their own may seem to be the only way to increase income and job satisfaction.

But you may not need to make such drastic changes in your lifestyle. You may just need to make some adjustments in your current situation. Unhappy at work? Worried about layoffs? Need a raise? Spend some time right now reviewing your contributions to the company. How can you make yourself indispensable? What do you do better than anyone else at work? Perhaps you are the fastest, or the most accurate, or the friendliest with the customers, or the most resourceful at solving problems. Believe it or not, your supervisor is not likely to be aware of these strengths! Employers and supervisors tend to see what is going wrong, rather than what is going right. It is up to you to make them aware of your valuable contributions.

Take twenty minutes to jot down every contribution you have made to your company. Ask a relative or co-worker to make a similar list about you—he or she may recognize strengths or remember incidents that you will have overlooked. Then organize this brainstorming list into a brief character sketch. You may surprise even yourself as you identify strengths and abilities you always took for granted.

After you have completed this meditation exercise, you might become so impressed with yourself that you may decide to put your assets to work for you. Do you have the personality to be your own boss? We discussed on Day 17 how hard you must work to get a business started. Now analyze yourself in terms of what kind of boss you would be.

Are you the type who motivates through encouragement, or do you criticize and belittle? Do you have the confidence to fire as well as hire when necessary? What if the employee is a family member or good friend? Will this hinder you from making valid business decisions?

Starting a Family Business

Your greatest asset should be as close as the dining room table. Each member of your family has skills, talents, and personality traits that are different from anyone else's. What about the personality of your family? As we discussed earlier, the advantages to starting a family business are numerous: an easily identified labor pool; the satisfaction of working together; an opportunity for children to earn money for college; a tax-advantaged asset that can be passed on to heirs easily; and flexible hours that can be adjusted for work load and family activities. But there are disadvantages, too: family members may not take the job seriously when they know they "can't" be fired; husbands and wives may find that the delicate balance of their marriage relationship is thrown off-kilter when one is boss, the other is employee; and still others may discover that instead of working at home, they are living at the office.

Today, assess the relationship you have with these potential employees: your family. Would a family business enhance that relationship or kill it? Where are your family members right now? Are they engaged in activities in the same room, or are they isolated behind closed doors? The answer to this question will help you assess the potential success of a family business.

Taking Advantage of Your Personal Assets

If, after this contemplation, you decide that self-employment is for you, take out the list of possible products that you began writing on Day 17 and review it. What could you sell? What are your personal interests and assets? My mother has the most beautiful flower gardens in all of Utah. Almost every year, her home wins awards for the beautiful landscaping. Each spring when she "divides" her irises, she sells the extra bulbs to eager customers. For years I have tried to convince her to start a consulting business, not to do gardening for others, but simply to share her artistic eye with them, telling her customers where, when, and which flowers to plant. You may have a similar talent that others would pay you to share.

Tap into Other People's Assets

Every day, you meet people who are successful in what they do. They may be wealthy businesspeople, dedicated mothers, school board members, Little League coaches, research librarians, or restaurant chefs. Tap into this valuable asset, your circle of friends and acquaintances. Listen to their conversations, especially their little gripes and complaints. Who would have thought, twenty years ago, that people would pay $50 an hour for a stranger to come into their homes to organize their closets and drawers? Yet these services are in high demand today. What other personal services could you turn into a business?

More important, develop these acquaintances as the core of your networking system. Whether you are looking for customers, suppliers, an investment partner, or just market ideas and information, your circle of friends is a valuable asset. Don't be a pest, but keep in touch through sending notes of interest or appreciation. Get to know your bank teller, postal worker, grocery clerk, and barber by name. You never know when one of these people will provide you with an important letter of introduction. Besides, being able to greet people by name gives you a sense of community that makes life worth living.

Your Greatest Asset: Knowledge

Perhaps your greatest asset is knowledge, especially knowledge of the world around you. Resolve to be more aware of events happening throughout the world. As you begin investing in the country funds you read about yesterday, you will find that your interest in those countries grows. You will want to know what is happening in China and Mexico, for example, because those events affect you. Consequently, your ability to make wise investment choices will increase—and that means more income and capital gains for you.

At the same time, as your knowledge of the culture and politics of these regions grows your personal worth will increase, making you an even more valued employee, parent, networking acquaintance, and public citizen. You're on your way to being independent, in more ways than one.

As you can see, you have many assets that don't appear on a bookkeeping ledger. You have interpersonal skills, reliability, entrepreneurship, family, friends, intelligence, and a thirst for greater knowledge. All these assets will help you increase your income and thus increase the quality of your life, not only so you can have more things, but so you can have a more satisfying and productive life.

ACTIONS TO TAKE ON DAY 21

1. Review ways to boost your take home pay by getting a raise at work.
2. Make a list of individuals who can teach you how to be more productive and a better investor.
3. Consider the benefits of self-employment or a family-operated business.
4. Boost your investment return by investing in aggressive growth companies and mutual funds, both here and abroad.

FOURTH WEEK:
Build Your Net Worth

HAVE A FINANCIAL CHECKUP II

Yesterday we counted your intangible blessings; today we are going to count your tangible ones. Remember when you were a kid, how much fun it was to sort and count your baseball cards, coin collection, money, and other treasures? Today we are going to do just that, but on a much grander scale. Over the next two days, we are going to discover what you are really worth financially.

When asked to list their net worth, most people quickly think of home, cars, investment accounts, and jewelry. Few consider other assets, such as furnishings, books, tools, sports equipment, and myriad other possessions acquired over a lifetime. Still others overlook the liabilities associated with their assets that reduce net worth—credit card balances, mortgages, auto loans, insurance fees, and the like. For now, let's ignore your liabilities and just add up all your assets. You may be surprised to discover how much you are really worth.

One woman I know, concerned about age and her approaching death, decided to inventory her belongings and make a will bequeathing each personal item to a specific heir. She had a large family and was concerned that bitter feelings might develop if they had to decide for themselves how to distribute her personal items. Moreover, she thought her heirs would appreciate her treasures more if they knew she had selected them personally and thoughtfully. Her list filled twenty pages! Not only was she happily surprised to discover how much she owned, but she also enjoyed the experience of deciding which of her family and friends would most enjoy receiving those items as a memento after her death.

Today we are not contemplating your will, but we are contemplating the pleasant surprise of discovering just how much you possess. Start with a looseleaf notebook and a large block of time. Divide the notebook into sections for such broad categories and subcategories as

- ◆ Fixed Assets
  House/condominium
  Second home
  Other (land, rental real estate)

- ◆ Investments
  Deposit/passbook accounts
  Checking accounts
  Life insurance policies
  Pension/401(k)/IRA/SEP
  Stocks and bonds
  Mutual funds
  Collectibles
  Other

♦ Moveable Assets
  Vehicles
  Furniture
  Boats/planes
  Tools
  Appliances
  Oriental rugs/antiques
  Art work

♦ Other
  Personal effects
  Jewelry
  Clothing
  Stereo/TV
  Musical instruments
  Cameras
  Collectibles
  China/silverware
  Sports equipment
  Other

Make several columns across each page, and label them with the following designations: Often, Regularly, Seldom, Never, Sentimental, Resale, Replace, Heir.

As you list each item you own, make marks in the appropriate columns. Some items you use often, every day, or every week. Others you use seldom but regularly, such as holiday dishes and decorations. Still others you may never use, but you may have strong sentimental attachment to them. Of course, you will probably discover several possessions that you never use and never intend to use. All of this information will be useful to you in tomorrow's exercise.

In the "resale" column list the amount you could get for each item if you had to sell it; in the "replacement" column, list the amount you would have to pay to replace it if it were lost, stolen, or broken. If you don't know these prices, leave that column blank for now. I'll tell you later in this chapter how to estimate values for both instances. Be aware that most people trick themselves into believing they are much richer than they really are by overestimating the current resale value of their personal possessions. Generally, 10 to 20 percent of the original purchase price is all you can expect to receive from your used personal items.

The final column, "Heir," is your gift list. Write the name of a friend or relative who you think would enjoy receiving this item someday. Not only will you have the enjoyment of giving something away without having to give it up now, but you will help your heirs avoid the curse of probate—bickering over such unique family treasures as Grandma's antique ring, Aunt Rita's original oil painting, Dad's '57 Chevy, or the Steinway Grand. In addition, you may decide to start giving some of these items as gifts now, substantially reducing your holiday expenditures at the same time. Of course, many of your possessions are simply utilitarian in nature and will simply be sold or given to charity someday. Leave the "Heir" column blank in those cases.

Listing Your Obvious Assets

List your obvious assets first: your real estate, cars, investment accounts, and so forth. Next, begin going through your home methodically, one room at a time. You may want to ask a trusted friend or relative to help you with this project, both to act as scribe and to offer advice. It will be time consuming, but a full inventory only needs to be done once. And it could be fun!

After your inventory is complete, it is time to organize the information. Keep the master list for yourself. Make a copy of the inventory, with estimated replacement values, for your insurance company. Send a notarized copy of the "gift list" to your attorney, to attach to your will. Then update this notebook annually or semiannually, using your No-Budget Budget list (see page 58) as a guide to help you review your acquisitions. It's as simple as that.

Finally, make an estimate of your gross assets, based on the resale value of the things you own. There are several ways to evaluate your assets, depending on the quality and condition of the item and on your urgency to sell. It is unfortunate but true that the more urgently you need to sell your possessions, the less money you are likely to get for them.

Your Investments

Let's begin with your cash. This is easy enough. Just add up your savings accounts, checking accounts, cookie jar stash, and any other cash in your possession. Next, do the same for your investments. Pull out your latest statements from your bank and brokerage accounts (such as your Automatic Investment Plan [AIP]), and see how much they are worth. If you have other investments besides those listed in your AIP statement, review those statements as well. Since most stocks and mutual funds are listed in the business section of the newspaper, it is easy—and advisable—to keep track of your investments every day.

Your Home

Next, let's evaluate your home. Again, we are just looking at gross figures today; tomorrow we will consider loans and other liabilities that detract from your net worth. If you live in a tract house in a large subdivision, coming up with a reliable estimate should be fairly easy. Simply get a printout of house sales over the past year, and check the comparables. Keep in mind, of course, that no two homes are identical. An upgraded kitchen, renovated family room, swimming pool, or cul-de-sac location will cause prices to vary among houses that started out identical.

Custom homes are harder to appraise and can be harder to sell as well. To get an approximate price, call a few real estate agents and ask them to give you a free appraisal. Don't pretend that you are thinking of selling right now. That isn't fair, and it isn't necessary. Most agents take a long-term view of client relations and are more than happy to give you a free appraisal, knowing that if you are pleased with their service, expertise, and demeanor, you will likely call them back when you are ready to sell. If the estimates given by two or three agents are reasonably close, simply take the average as your estimated gross value. If the appraisals vary widely, get a few more estimates and ask for a more detailed explanation of how the agents arrived at their assessments. One may be aware of a condition or situation that the other overlooked. You could hire a professional appraiser, too, but unless you are serious about selling within the next six months, this is an unnecessary expense.

Your Vehicles

Discovering the resale value of your automobile can rank as one of the most disappointing experiences in life. If you follow the advice we discussed on Day 11 about how to save money by buying a used car, your next resale won't have to be so disappointing. Meanwhile, let's determine how much your current vehicles are worth:

♦ Check the classified section of your daily paper and see how much others are asking for similar makes and models. Year, options, and mileage are the most important variables to match. Call some of the sellers, and ask what kind of response they are getting to their ads. This will probably give you the most accurate estimate of how much your car is currently worth to potential buyers in your community.

♦ Check the price of your car in the National Automobile Dealers Association Blue Book, which will provide you with the estimated wholesale value.

♦ You could also visit a few car dealers to get an idea of how much they would give you for the car. This is the most foolish way to sell a car, since the dealer must offer you a middleman price, in anticipation of reselling it at a higher price. But it will give you an idea of the true cash value you could expect for a quick disposal. Don't ask for a trade-in value; this would give you a price distorted by the dealer's anticipation of haggling over the purchase price of the new car for which you would be trading in your car. Make it clear that you are simply looking for a "here and now" price for your car.

Jewelry and Other Valuables

The classifieds are a good source of information for evaluating all your possessions. Look for comparable items, and see what price is being asked. If prices vary widely, call sellers and ask if their items have sold. Don't be a pest—be short, pleasant, and appreciative when asking for this information.

Pawnshops, estate buyers, and auction houses are additional sources of information. They will give you written appraisals, but the appraisals are binding for just one day.

Unfortunately, you will find that many of your possessions have very little resale value. This should tell you three things:

♦ Think twice before you purchase consumer goods.

♦ Don't consider consumer purchases to be investments.

♦ When you do buy, select items of high quality that tend to retain their value.

When buying jewelry, for example, don't buy anything less than 18- or 22-carat gold. The higher the carat, the purer the gold and hence the better the price you will receive if you decide to sell. The proliferation of 14-carat gold in the United States and in Europe has left many a family with possessions that are worth little more than their sentimental value. When you buy gold jewelry, make sure you are paying for the weight, not for the artistic design, by buying directly from a goldsmith. I remember buying some 22-

carat gold bracelets for my wife from a goldsmith in Toronto. I paid less than 5 percent over the spot price of gold that day. Meanwhile, beautifully designed 14-carat bracelets were selling for twice the price in retail jewelry stores I visited before I left home.

The question here is not one of frugality but of value. As I have repeated throughout this book I have nothing against spending money, just against spending money unwisely.

Antiques and Furniture

Antiques and collectible knickknacks are much more difficult to evaluate because the market is so volatile. Several antique guides are available at your local library but chances are they won't give you an accurate price because with antiques and collectibles, each item is unique. Your best bet, if you have some extremely fine pieces, is to hire an antiques appraiser. This may cost $200 or more, but if you have a large collection, it's worth the cost, both for establishing your net worth and for keeping your insurance information current.

Ordinary items like contemporary furniture, appliances, decorative furnishings, dishes, and such should be valued at no more than 10 percent of your original purchase price. This may seem shocking, but the market for these types of items is so large and plentiful that resale prices plummet to dismally low levels. Since the purpose of this exercise is to establish an immediate liquidation value of your assets, you need to assume a rock-bottom price. Browse through a few garage sales this weekend to see what your everyday items might be worth.

Now, pull out your calculator and start adding up the resale columns in your inventory notebook. What do you think of the total of your gross assets? Is it more than you expected, less than you had hoped, or about what you thought it would be? Sleep peacefully tonight as you contemplate your vast empire. Tomorrow we will begin evaluating the other side of the ledger, your liabilities.

ACTIONS TO TAKE ON DAY 22

1. Go through your house and list all your personal items, especially those with sentimental value. Invite a relative or friend to join you in this exercise.

2. Determine the value of all your liquid assets, including bank and brokerage accounts.

3. Determine the value of your house and other real estate.

4. Estimate the resale value of your automobiles and other movable assets.

5. Using your calculator, add up the estimated value of all your assets.

DAY 23

TURN YOUR LIABILITIES INTO ASSETS

After making yesterday's list of assets, you are probably feeling pretty wealthy. Even at discounted resale prices, your possessions could generate a great deal of cash if you decided to sell them. But have you considered the other side of the ledger, your liabilities?

Let's look at your most valuable asset, your home. You may know for certain that your neighbors sold an identical house down the street six months ago for $250,000. But as you probably know, that doesn't mean that you could walk away from a similar sale with a quarter of a million dollars in your pocket. Real estate commissions, settlement fees, and other closing costs could take as much as 10 to 15 percent. Capital gains taxes could take as much as 28 percent more if you need to use that cash for something besides another personal residence. In addition, the balance of your mortgage will be deducted from the sales price. If you have borrowed heavily against the equity in your home, you may not have an asset at all.

An asset is something you own or control that generates wealth. Some assets, like your residence or a piece of art, are passive; they don't generate wealth until you actually sell them. Others, like dividend-paying stocks or rental real estate, generate income even while you own them. Yet both are considered assets because they can be converted to cash.

But, while all sellable possessions can be considered assets, not all assets should be considered investments. You may own several possessions that you could sell for cash, as you discovered during your inventory yesterday. Your cars or stereo equipment, for example, could generate several thousand dollars. But these items cannot be accurately described as investments unless you could sell them for a profit. If you have to sell these possessions at a discounted price, you could hardly call them wise investments. An asset can only be called an investment if it generates income or if it can be sold for a profit. Keep this in mind as we evaluate your liabilities today.

Some liabilities are fixed and current, while others are temporary, variable, or anticipated in the future. For example, your mortgage, car payments, business loans, and home-equity loans are fixed and permanent for the life of the loan. On the other hand, credit cards and other consumer debts vary from month to month. Money to be used for college tuition may be listed as an asset right now, while you are still saving, but it needs to be listed as an anticipated liability on your ledger, since that money is already spoken for. Other anticipated expenditures include orthodontia, your next car, retirement costs, family vacations, and other specific goals for which your savings are earmarked.

Monthly living expenses should be listed as a liability, too, just as monthly income is listed as an asset. Determine your average costs for utilities, groceries, insurance, gas, entertainment, clothes, and so forth by reviewing your No-Budget Budget and deduct that amount from your anticipated income to determine the net worth of your salary.

A list of liabilities and expenses might include the following:

LIABILITIES AND EXPENSES

Housing Costs
   Rent/mortgage
   Mortgage insurance
   Homeowner's insurance
   Taxes and condo or homeowner association fees
   Utilities/telephone
Living Expenses
   Life insurance premiums
   Medical/dental
   Clothing
   Groceries
   Other
Financial
   Rent-to-own payments
   Personal loans
   Home-equity loan (if not included above)
   Credit cards
   Account maintenance fees (IRA/401(k)/SEP)
   Legal fees
   Accounting fees
   Other
Miscellaneous
   College tuition
   Student loans
   Private school fees
   Legal judgments
   Alimony/child support
   Other

Figuring Your Net Worth

Now total your liabilities and deduct them from your assets. The result may astound you. It is not unusual for many people to discover that they actually have a negative net worth. Despite all the gadgets and possessions that fill their homes and driveways, they actually owe more than they own. If you are among those people, don't despair! The principles you are learning this month as you read and study this book will turn your life around, and by this time next year you will be filling your ledgers with black ink instead of red.

For now, let's see how we can turn your negative balance into a positive one. As I explained above, an asset is only an asset if it is providing some kind of benefit for you that compensates for the attached liability. This principle applies whether the benefit is financial, such as interest on an investment; physical, such as the shelter and security you receive from your home; or less quantifiable, such as the added productivity you gain from owning a home computer. These benefits must be weighed against their attached liabilities, however, before you can make an accurate assessment of their true worth.

For example, suppose you bought a pleasure boat ten years ago for $20,000. It was great fun while the kids were teenagers, but now they're grown and you use the boat only once or twice a year. Do you still consider it an asset?

Since the boat is fully paid for, and you could sell it for a few hundred dollars, it may seem to be an asset. But what about the costs that accrue in the meantime? While the boat sits idle month after month, you are still required to pay for insurance, basic maintenance, dock and/or marina fees, county tags and licensing, and depreciation. Wouldn't it make more sense to sell the boat, invest the proceeds, and rent a shiny new boat once or twice a year when families come to visit? Instead of reducing your standard of living, selling your asset in this case would increase your joy in living.

This same principle applies to other so-called assets that you may own. Unless they are serving a useful purpose, they may need to be sold, given away, or thrown out.

Look through the list of assets you compiled yesterday, and review your assessments of how often you use each item and whether it has sentimental value. Now consider the liabilities associated with ownership of each possession: storage, insurance, maintenance, and payments, for example. I knew of one retired couple, living alone in a 4,500-square-foot house. Why? Because they had accumulated so much stuff over their lifetime that they couldn't fit into a smaller, less expensive home. They never realized how much they were paying in storage fees!

Invite a Friend

It may help to have another person go through the list with you to help you release your emotional attachment to unnecessary possessions, especially if you have a pack rat personality. You could ask a trusted friend or relative, or you could hire a "closet consultant" trained in this kind of personal organization.

Periodically, my wife goes through our children's rooms, armed with several trash bags and collection boxes. She gives the children ample warning so they have time to put away the things they really want to keep. Then Jo Ann cleans like a demon, eliminating toys, clothes, and knickknacks that have neither intrinsic nor sentimental value. Over the years she has become quite proficient at knowing what to keep and what to toss. By the end of the day she has a pile for the charity garage sale, a pile for hand-me-downs, and a pile for the garbage collector. The rooms are clean again, and the children are secretly relieved that they didn't have to do the agonizing tossing themselves. We have a nice tax deduction, and the church youth group has money from its parking lot garage sale. As the children have grown older, they have learned to do this "spring cleaning" themselves, often selling their discarded possessions to neighborhood friends for cash instead of donating them to charity—our kids aren't interested in tax deductions yet!

You can begin a similar spring cleaning of your entire house. But beware of becoming overly exuberant at first. We had a friend in college who would look through her closet every few months and become angry at herself for having wasted so much money on clothing and accessories. As punishment, she would have an apartment sale, offering all her things for 10 percent of her purchase price. Of course, the next day seller's regret would kick in as she realized that she literally had nothing to wear. Then she would run to the department store, and the cycle would begin again.

To avoid seller's regret, go slowly at first. This exercise is not meant to make you throw away your prized possessions simply because they have no real monetary value. If you have an emotional or sentimental attachment to an item, don't get rid of it. Your aim is just to increase the efficiency of your financial portfolio. Make your piles of potential discards, then allow your family veto rights before you actually sell their possessions. Discuss the value of each asset from a financial and a sentimental perspective. If the asset is still wanted by a majority of family members, then keep it. But don't allow them simply to cart the items back to their closets! Plan a cooling-off period of a month or so and a cooling-off place, like the garage. Discuss the liabilities involved with keeping the items—storage, maintenance, insurance—and the potential benefits of eliminating them—cash and space. If at the end of the cooling-off period the items are still not being used, you can sell them with a clear conscience.

Sources of Selling

How should you market these discarded possessions?

Several sources exist. Use the techniques we discussed earlier such as garage sales (Day 5) and classified advertisements (Day 12). For personal items like clothing and accessories, you may wish to use the service of a consignment shop. For cars and boats, consider an advertisement in your local auto/boat trader.

For fine art and other collectibles, contact an auction house, such as Sotheby's or Christie's in New York.

Tools, sports equipment, furniture, and electronics will garner the highest prices by selling them through the classifieds. Accentuate the positive in your ad, of course, but be honest in your description. Saying that a beat-up stereo is "like new" may encourage a high volume of callers, but buyers become disgruntled when they learn the truth about the stereo's condition, wasting their time and yours. To establish a fair price, look at ads for comparable items and set a price near the high side of the range. You can always negotiate downward.

Automobiles, trailers, and boats will also capture the highest price through the classified ads. With such a high ticket item, it is worth investing a little time and money into fixing the vehicle up for sale. Americans tend to be emotionally attached to their cars and boats; they want transportation that looks and feels good, too. Consequently, the better a car or boat looks, the more eager the customer will be to buy. For one hundred dollars or so you can have your car "detailed"—washed and waxed inside and out till it looks almost brand new. Potential buyers will be dazzled by the sparkling exterior even before they give it a test drive. And if you just happen to schedule two or three callers to look at the car at the same time, you may enjoy a nice little bidding war in your driveway.

Sell Your House for More Than It's Worth

Homes, too, sell faster when they look better and when potential buyers are aware of their competition. Interview two or three agents before selecting one to use as your listing agent. Ask each one about advertising plans, experience in the neighborhood, price range, and potential buyers they may already be working with. Even though you must ultimately choose one agent, the others will begin thinking of buyers to bring to your house, and they will be ready when you are to show your house.

The three essential keys to selling a house for the highest price are making it look good, asking a reasonable price, and selling it fast. Before listing your house for sale, have it thoroughly cleaned, including windows and woodwork. If possible, store window screens in the garage temporarily to improve the view. Add some flowers and shrubbery if appropriate, and keep the yard well manicured. Don't allow early birds to see the house until you have it ready for its grand opening. Then schedule as many lookers as possible for the first weekend. You want to create the impression of a hot property about to be snapped up.

Contact all the agents you interviewed, and tell them you are ready for them to show the house. If you were cordial and businesslike during the interviews, called back to thank them for their efforts, explained why you chose someone else, and invited them to show the house anyway, they will not be offended. Establish a price only slightly above the appraisal price—no more than 5 percent. You will get more serious buyers if the price is right, and you won't have to negotiate as much if buyers are aware that others are looking at the house that same weekend. When an offer comes in the first week, don't get greedy, thinking that you should have asked more. The early offer is a reflection of your careful marketing preparation, not a too-low price. The appraisal price is a fair price for everyone. I have known of too many people who rejected an early offer, only to regret that decision months later, when they finally settled on a sales price 10 or 20 percent lower.

Charitable Giving

Sometimes a tax deduction can be worth more than cash.

Remember Bill Clinton's $3 used boxer shorts? If you can't sell your losing assets, you should consider giving them away. These assets may not have a use for you, but they can still be useful to others. Donate these goods to a charity, such as Goodwill or the

Salvation Army. Obtain an official receipt for the items you donate and list the receipt as a charitable deduction when you file your income tax return. This action will help in reducing your tax liability while helping out a needy organization.

ACTIONS TO TAKE ON DAY 23

1. List your liabilities and deduct them from your gross assets to discover your net worth.
2. Evaluate which assets are costing you money and decide to sell them if appropriate.
3. Eliminate useless goods through garage sales, classified ads, or donations.

CONTROL YOUR DEBTS

Few things in life can cause individuals and families more stress and dissension than debt. Regardless of who you are or how wealthy, at some point in your life, you will have to cope with a debt crisis. If you are lucky, that crisis will come early enough and intensely enough to forestall future debt crises. Tomorrow we'll examine ways to get you out of debt without losing your livelihood and your credit rating. Today, however, we'll look at how to avoid accumulating debt in the first place.

This chapter could be summed up in one simple statement: Cancel all your credit cards, and pay cash for everything. But I recognize that avoiding debt isn't as easy as that. If it were, Americans would not have filed a million bankruptcies last year. Still, there are ways to control consumer spending and consumer debt

so that you can avoid the debtors' prison many Americans create
for themselves.

Americans are falling further and further into the mire of consumer debt. In 1975, consumer debt ate up 67 percent of disposable
income. The figure rose to 75 percent in 1980, 80 percent in 1985,
and 97 percent in 1990. How did we get into this mess in the first
place? One reason is obvious: Americans want more than they can
afford, and they want it now. Parents, obsessed with giving their
children the "perfect childhood," worry that if they make Joey wait
for his swing set, trampoline, pitching machine, or battery-powered
car until they can afford it, he will have outgrown the desire for it
and they will miss out on the pleasure of watching him enjoy it.
Young adults agonize that by the time they can afford to travel, they
will be too old to enjoy it. Others rationalize that designer clothes
and luxury cars will enhance their status and give them an edge in
the business world. Few are willing to wait any more. We have
become a society that demands instant gratification.

The Lure of Easy Credit

Another factor leading to the crisis in debt is the ease with
which credit cards can be obtained. Banks and department stores
make it incredibly easy to buy on "credit." (In today's upside-down
world, spending is called saving, consumer goods are called investments, and debt is called credit!) In fact, department store sales
clerks are instructed to urge every customer to open a charge
account, and they receive a commission for every application they
successfully complete. Nearly every week you receive a letter from
yet another bank, offering you a credit card with a preauthorized
limit. Resisting such offers becomes increasingly difficult, especially when your checking account balance is low.

Social acceptability of indebtedness has made debt accumulation easier, too. There was a time when Americans were embarrassed by debt. One of my favorite lines from Harper Lee's *To Kill
a Mockingbird* is Mrs. Dubose's noble assertion, "I don't want to

die beholden to anything." But few people have such concerns about social stigma, if such a thing exists today. For, in fact, it has become almost a status symbol to brag about having a high credit card balance, I suppose because it indicates that your income qualifies you for such a high credit limit.

Recently, I overheard some parents in the little league bleachers laughing about their debts. One said to the others, "In our first decade of marriage, the credit card bill was three figures; in our second decade it was four figures. We celebrated our twentieth anniversary last year, so naturally we're into five figures now." The other parents laughingly agreed. I was appalled, not only by the size of their consumer debts, but by their cavalier attitude toward it. Far from looking down on those who must borrow, today we are expected to admire those who qualify for a gold or platinum card.

Additionally, the government itself has for years encouraged debt accumulation, rewarding those who borrow with tax deductions while taxing those who save. Interest on consumer debts is no longer tax deductible, but by using a home-equity loan to pay off your credit cards, you can easily make those debts tax deductible.

I admit that some debts are acceptable and will not ruin your financial independence. Home mortgages, business loans, investing on margin, education costs, and perhaps a car loan can all be seen as acceptable reasons to borrow money. After all, you can't get a job without an education, and you can't get to work without a car. But buying with borrowed money can make it too easy to buy more than you need. If you budget $300 a month over three years for a mid-size car, what's to stop you from paying $350 a month over five years for a luxury car? It seems as if the nicer car is costing you only $50 extra, not $10,200.

Today's Exercise

Sometimes facing your debts head-on is a good way to start facing them down. Pull out your credit card statements for the past five years. How many items are you still paying for that have absolutely no current value to you? Your statements may include clothing that is out of style or no longer fits; restaurant dinners; Christmas presents; theater tickets; and amusement parks. You may even have sold an item you no longer use for less money than it is still costing you! Debt is like prison: Consumers become trapped by previous decisions, unable to make choices today because last year's choices have already laid claim to their future income.

The techniques and principles you have read about in this book will help you avoid similar entrapment in the future, because you are becoming a wiser consumer. For the rest of today, we will examine ways to continue using the acceptable benefits of plastic instead of money while avoiding debt.

When Is Debt Legitimate?

Despite the warnings mentioned above, there are legitimate reasons to use plastic instead of cash. First, it is safer than carrying large sums of cash that could be lost or stolen. Second, it establishes a record of your spending and a second receipt that comes to your house in one convenient statement. Third, it allows you to order items over the phone, hold reservations at hotels and theaters, and rent everything from cars to video movies without having to put down a cash deposit. Fourth, it gives you additional recourse in case you are dissatisfied with an item or service you purchase. Fifth, it establishes a credit history, which you will need if you want to borrow money for a house, car, business, or other useful purpose someday.

A Great Alternative

The best way to enjoy these benefits without incurring debt is to use a *debit* card. Debit cards look exactly like credit cards and are accepted by many merchants just as readily. The difference is that instead of having to pay the bank at the end of the month for all the items you purchased, the funds are immediately withdrawn from your checking account and paid to the merchant. In essence, the debit card is a plastic checkbook, part of that new cashless society that everyone was talking about ten years ago. The merchant simply swipes your debit card—usually the same card you use to withdraw money from your automatic teller machine (ATM)—through a terminal, and you enter your personal identification number for verification. With the advent of fiber-optic networks and the increased efficiency of long-distance lines, you can now use your debit card almost anywhere in the country.

If few merchants in your area have installed the special terminals for use with ATM debit cards, you can still use a debit card to have money withdrawn directly from your bank account. Visa and Mastercard issue a type of debit card that can be used anywhere that credit cards are accepted. Get started today by calling your bank or broker for a debit card application.

The advantages of a debit card are many. It can be used as easily as a credit card. It is accepted for phone purchases and rental deposits. It provides a monthly statement. And it prevents the problem of bounced checks, since the purchase will be rejected if you do not have sufficient funds to cover the amount. One drawback is that it is easy to lose track of your account balance when you use a debit card instead of handwritten checks. Eventually I expect cards will come with a microchip that maintains your account balance for you, but until then, get into the habit of recording all your debit card purchases and deducting them from your checking account balance.

Carry a Charge Card

You may have a legitimate need for a credit card, especially if you own a business or work for a company that reimburses you once a month for expenses you incur on the job. But to avoid the temptation to spend the reimbursement and carry the credit card charges, I recommend that you use a charge card instead of a credit card. What is the difference? Credit card companies allow you to pay just a portion of the outstanding balance each month, sometimes less than 10 percent. At 18 percent interest or more, this "convenience" can add up to big expenses. Charge cards, on the other hand, require that the balance be paid in full every month. With some prearranged exceptions—vacation travel, for example—you cannot use a charge card to borrow money for more than a month. Consequently, you can enjoy the convenience and help of short-term borrowing without the risk of long-term debt. American Express, Diner's Club, and Carte Blanche are some examples of charge cards. Each charges an annual fee to own a card, and interest will accrue if you are late in paying the bill.

If You Must Use Credit Cards...

Of course, a no-annual fee credit card is acceptable if you have the discipline to pay the bill off each month. I have painted a pretty bleak picture of credit card use, because it causes trouble for so many people. But others of us manage to use credit cards regularly without going into debt. One secret to debt management is to keep a running total of your credit card expenditures, just as you do your checkbook expenditures. That way, you know precisely how much your bill will be and can plan accordingly. To prevent overspending, I recommend that you deduct your credit purchases directly from your checkbook as you buy them. Then write a single check to your credit card company when the bill comes. (Double-check your figures to see that they match, and make sure you don't deduct the items twice from your check register.)

Interest rates and annual fees vary widely, so choose the credit card that will cost you the least. Even if you always pay your bill in full, there will be times when interest charges will accrue—a check gets lost in the mail, an emergency causes you to be late sending the payment, or an unexpected hardship makes you miss a payment.

I have found five institutions that charge less than 11.9 percent for the money they lend through credit cards. The lowest charges a mere 8 percent! That's a savings of over 60 percent over the typical 19.8 percent rate. On a credit card balance of $10,000, the savings is almost $1,200 per year.

The following is a list of the five lowest interest credit cards and their phone numbers. My favorite variable interest card is issued by Arkansas Federal. Their 8 percent variable rate card is pegged to the prime rate, so the rate will fluctuate. For fixed rates, my choice is Peoples Bank of Bridgeport, which is offering an 11.5 percent fixed rate with a $25 annual fee.

Each one of these credit cards has a twenty-five day grace period, so you can pay off the entire balance each month without penalty or interest charge.

The Five Lowest Rate Credit Cards

Simmons First National Bank
Pine Bluff, Arkansas
Call 800-636-5151 for an application
8.5 percent variable rate, $35 annual fee

Arkansas Federal Credit Card Services
Little Rock, Arkansas
Call 800-477-3348 for an application
9 percent variable rate, $35 annual fee

Wachovia
Wilmington, Delaware
Call 800-842-3262 for an application
Prime rate for the first year, then prime plus 3.9 percent variable rate, $39 annual fee

Oak Brook Bank
Oak Brook, Illinois

Call 800-666-1011 for an application
Prime for the first year, after that 12.1 percent with $27
annual fee or 13.15 percent variable, with no annual fee

Peoples Bank of Bridgeport
Bridgeport, Connecticut
Call 800-423-3273 for an application
11.5 percent fixed, $25 annual fee

Lower credit card rates are also available from credit unions. If you belong to a credit union, then you should investigate its rates. On average, credit union rates are 4 percent to 6 percent less than the highest rate cards.

Before sending away for a new card, call or write to your current company and tell them you are shopping around for lower rates. They may be willing to reduce your rate in order to keep you as a customer.

Why would they make such an offer, especially if you pay the bill in full every month and thus never send them any interest payments? How can you be considered a "valued customer" if you never "buy" their credit? Credit card companies earn money two ways: through the interest payments and annual fees paid by cardholders, and through the commissions paid to them by merchants, as much as 4 percent of the purchase price. If you are a steady customer with a clean credit history, they won't want to lose you, even if you never pay them a dime in interest, because they are already collecting 4 percent of your monthly total from the merchants.

Affinity Cards

Many banks offer "affinity cards" now. These are credit cards tied to other companies that offer special promotions and bonuses for your businesses. Major airlines award frequent flyer miles for every dollar purchased on their affinity credit card, for example. Similarly, General Motors issues a lower rate, no-annual-fee credit card tied to a rebate toward a General Motors car based upon card usage. If you're in the market for a car in about two or three years or if you travel frequently, one of these cards may help reduce your costs.

But, there is danger in using these affinity cards. You may begin using it for all your ordinary expenses with the intent of paying it off in full each month, just to increase your bonus miles. Meanwhile, your checking account appears fuller than usual, so the pressure to avoid impulse spending lessens and you soon find yourself trapped by installment credit. As we'll find out later this week, credit cards have a way of ruining your finances in a hurry. They are just too convenient. Better put a barrier between yourself and easy credit.

Establishing a Credit History—Safely

If you are just starting out and need to establish a credit history, the best and safest kind of card is one issued by a gasoline company. The amount you drive tends to be governed by your actual transportation needs, not by the availability of gas money, so you aren't as subject to impulse spending with a gas card as with an all-purpose credit card. (But be careful of the convenience stores associated with gas stations these days!)

Till Debt Do Us Part

Excessive debt is usually a family problem. It affects all aspects of life, making even the most trivial purchases seem difficult when the bulk of the family income must be spent to pay bills for goods and services used long ago. Debt is an unforgiving specter that hangs over the lives of millions of people. When faced with seemingly insurmountable debts many people simply give up. It is becoming all too common for Americans to say, "I'm going to buy everything I can until they take away my credit cards. Then I'll declare bankruptcy and start over." Unfortunately, starting over means going back beyond "Square One," to a hole deeper than you realized. It can take decades to dig your way out.

Examine your reasons for debt accumulation. The techniques we described in the No-Budget Budget will help you curb the impulse spending that leads to so much consumer debt. Canceling your credit cards will help even more, although it may be extremely difficult to do that right away, if most of your income each month is being used to pay the bills from last month's expenditures. If your addiction to credit card spending is overwhelming, you may need to spend some time with a psychologist, finding ways to rechannel that need.

You must take the opportunity, while you are able to earn money, to reduce your debts to zero. This should be your family's goal. It is possible, and the rewards of a debt-free life are immense. Each time you reduce your debt by one dollar, you have one more dollar to invest. It is time to make the power of compounding work for you, instead of against you!

ACTIONS TO TAKE ON DAY 24

1. Evaluate your debt patterns by reviewing your credit card records for the past two to three years.
2. Learn to avoid accumulating debt by switching to a debit card or charge card.
3. Consider cutting up your credit cards.

GET OUT OF DEBT WITHOUT
FILING FOR BANKRUPTCY

It may seem obvious, but it bears repeating: The best way to live debt free is to avoid borrowing in the first place. But for most Americans, that option is long gone. Debt has already become an unbearable burden. Current income is already spoken for, with almost nothing left for this month's needs after last month's bills are paid. I see people buying groceries with their Visa cards and making car payments with their cash advance checks. The cycle seems endless, and the hole just gets deeper. Debt has become their master, and they often look to bankruptcy as their savior.

But as we shall see, bankruptcy does not lead to financial salvation. It simply provides a temporary respite, while the storm gathers strength to pummel you again. Today we will examine ways to liberate yourself from this self-made debtors' prison, in a way that will keep you from becoming a repeat offender.

The Inside Scoop on Collection Agencies

If you have experienced debt problems in the past or if bill collectors are knocking at your door right now, you know that the worst part of owing money is having to deal with collection agencies. Their job is to get you to pay, and they know that the surest way to do so is to intimidate you. It can be an agonizing, demeaning, painful experience, full of emotional turmoil.

But collection agencies are just another business. Mean and uncaring though they may seem, they really aren't the bad guys. They simply act as the middleman between the creditor and the debtor, enforcing a contract that the debtor voluntarily signed. By the time your account has reached a collection agency, it has been through the creditors' own in-house collectors, and you have had numerous opportunities to explain legitimate discrepancies and reasons for not paying. Now it is time to honor the contract. But what if you don't have that much money?

Intimidation is the bill collector's greatest tool. Often, all it takes is a letter from a collection agency threatening legal action to convince debtors to pay up. Intimidation tactics used by bill collectors used to be onerous: calls in the middle of the night, visits to your office, verbal abuse. But collection agencies today are bound by certain laws that prohibit them from:

- ◆ harassing, threatening, or verbally abusing debtors
- ◆ implying that they are attorneys, private investigators, or representatives of credit bureaus
- ◆ contacting you by phone before 8 a.m. or after 9 p.m.

♦ informing anyone else, including your employer, that you owe money

♦ contacting anyone else except to inquire about your whereabouts

♦ contacting you again if you inform them in writing to cease. (But beware, writing such a cease-and-desist letter will cause the creditor to start legal action against you, an event you want to avoid since it reduces your power to negotiate.)

Unfortunately, some agencies will break these laws to frighten you into paying. If that is the case, contact the Federal Trade Commission's Consumer Protection Bureau, Credit Practices Division, Washington, D.C. 20580, 202-326-2222.

Making the Collection Agency Work for You

Collection agencies are usually paid a commission based on the amount actually collected. If they collect nothing, they are paid nothing. If they collect a portion, they are paid a percentage of that portion. This gives the collector an incentive to collect any amount, including a reduced settlement. It also gives them an incentive to close the deal fast, since they aren't paid an hourly wage. This can be used to your advantage.

The collection agency has the power to negotiate the claim with you, so use the opportunity to negotiate, negotiate, negotiate, negotiate. Don't become emotional, and don't get into a shouting match. The bill collector doesn't need to know your personal problems. His job is simply to close the case. In a way he is working for you, as well as for the creditor, because isn't closing the case and getting on with your life your goal, too?

Work together to arrive at a solution. You can almost always have interest charges dropped or at least suspended if you set up a workable payment plan, and you can usually get a portion of the principle amount waived as well. Your margin for negotiation will be influenced by whether your loan is "secured" or "unsecured." Any debts that are guaranteed by a physical asset, such as your house, car, or bank account, are considered secured. This means that if you default on the loan, the creditor gains possession of the item used to secure it, called the collateral. If the collateral is worth more than the outstanding balance, your power to negotiate is limited. If it is worth less, then you can usually offer to pay the book price of the collateral, thus saving the creditor the time and expense of selling the repossessed item. Unsecured loans have no collateral. They are issued strictly on the basis of your credit status and your promise (the signature) to pay. Credit cards and most personal loans are unsecured. Because the creditor has nothing to repossess, he is more likely to negotiate for a discounted repayment.

The sooner your creditors can close the case, the more willing they will be to discount your payoff amount. Their motivation to close will be even greater if you are on the brink of declaring bankruptcy, since that would virtually eliminate their opportunity to collect. Here is a suggestion on how to handle the negotiations:

- ♦ Admit that you owe the money and are willing to pay it back, but you just don't have it all right now. This signals to the collector that you are willing to work with him to solve the problem and that you will not be setting up an adversarial relationship.

- ♦ Tell the collector how much you can afford to pay, and when you will be able to pay it. Ask to set up an extended payment plan by which you can pay a little each month, but without interest charges accruing. This concession alone could make it possible for you to get out of debt, as it is the continued stockpiling of interest that makes the task insurmountable. Most companies will agree to waive interest charges at this point.

- ♦ If you have some extra money from a tax refund, employment bonus, or second job, negotiate a low one-time payment to wipe off the entire debt. If the company has already written you off the books as a bad debt, it will treat payment as "found money."

Ask for the agreement in writing, and when you have fulfilled your terms, request a statement that payment has been made in full.

As you can see, you have a surprising amount of control in this collection process, and you can use it to your advantage. Ultimately, however, it is up to your creditor to decide whether to grant you leniency. You did sign a contract to pay, and you have a moral obligation to do so unless the creditor willingly reduces that amount.

The B Word

What about bankruptcy? Isn't that the easiest way to get out of debt and start over with a clean slate? Thanks to a law passed in 1978, it has become easier than ever to get out of debt through the bankruptcy process. Today's bankruptcy law is very kind to the debtor, and almost merciless to the creditor. It allows debtors to keep more personal property, including their personal residence. In fact, bankrupts can live an almost normal life after bankruptcy, as long as they are content with paying cash for about seven to ten years. And today, there are even loan institutions that specialize in providing credit to bankrupts right away. No one even needs to know—except the creditors whose bills you won't be paying and you.

Look on the shelf in any library or bookstore and you will find dozens of how-to books on bankruptcy. It has become acceptable, even fashionable, for Americans to file. In fact, many lenders have adapted their services to accommodate the bankrupt consumer, developing a new category for his spending needs. You may have become a bad credit risk, but if you're willing to pay 25 percent or

30 percent interest, you can still buy almost anything. Check the classified ads for car sales and you'll see dealer ads beckoning one and all to buy a car, regardless of financial situation. Bad credit? Bankruptcy? No problem, they promise.

The False Lure of Bankruptcy

If you want information on how to file, you're reading the wrong book. I firmly believe that filing for bankruptcy is a cop-out, an illegitimate flight from legitimate debts. Bankruptcy may be legal, but that doesn't mean it is right. There are consequences to your decision not to repay your debts, consequences that affect more than your own credit rating. For one thing, every dollar you decide not to repay returns as a higher cost for legitimate consumers like myself, as businesses try to compensate for their losses. I'm not going to help you do that.

More important, bankruptcy tends to breed bankruptcy. A few years ago, I learned that a business associate was considering bankruptcy. He was a coin dealer, and as a result of his filing, he was not sending coins to customers who had already paid him. Incensed, I called him on the phone and asked how he could make such an unethical decision. What about his customers? His answer astounded me. He was distraught. He did not want to declare bankruptcy; he was proud of the business he had built over the years and valued the reputation he had earned. But one of his own suppliers had just declared bankruptcy, refusing to deliver a huge contract of coins for which he had paid nearly a million dollars in advance. Now he had no coins, no money, and a list of angry customers who were now his unhappy creditors.

Perhaps if I had searched further, I would have discovered an even earlier bankruptcy that had precipitated the supplier's filing. Bankruptcy often causes a domino effect, tumbling the delicate financial balance of businesses and individuals in both directions. I would never encourage someone to take part in the toppling.

Bankruptcy, moreover, is just a temporary cure, a Band-Aid where major surgery is required. Unless you make fundamental changes in the way you handle money, bankruptcy only provides a temporary respite from your financial ills. The actions that have put you in this position frequently remain, and in many cases, families and individuals who have filed for bankruptcy find themselves back in the same sinking ship of debt just a couple of years later. You must overcome the misuse of debt first, but that will never happen until you experience the full consequences.

If bankruptcy is currently in your plans, I strongly urge you to reconsider. It is an irresponsible act of deceit against a business that has already honored its end of the bargain. Bankruptcy may be legally and even socially acceptable, but it is not ethical. Moreover, as you are about to discover, it is not even necessary. Debt can be controlled and eliminated without pushing your creditors to the brink of bankruptcy with you.

The Honorable Way to Eliminate Debts

Follow these simple steps to eliminate debt:

♦ Organize your debts into a single list, and keep track of your running balances in a ledger. Do not consolidate your loans, however.

♦ Contact your creditors, and ask them to be patient while you work to pay off their debts. Use the techniques described above to reduce the principle and eliminate interest, if possible.

♦ Ask service providers to reduce your debt, if appropriate. For example, some doctors will readjust their bills for clients whose income and personal situation make it impossible to pay the full amount. But remember, this is a request, not a demand. It is up to the provider to decide whether to forgive part of your debt.

♦ Consider contacting a credit counselor to help you arrange a payment plan. He will use the same techniques I have described above, but sometimes creditors are more willing to give concessions if they are dealing with a credit counseling agency they already know and trust.

♦ Pay the minimum required for each of your debt obligations, and then pay extra on the debts that charge the highest interest.

♦ Pay off your smallest debts first, to enjoy the satisfaction of crossing them completely off your list.

♦ Reduce expenditures to the barest necessities. Later, when you are out of debt, use cash to buy the things you need so you never have to go through this again.

♦ Take on extra jobs, and use all the money to pay off your debts. Encourage all family members to participate. After all, the children helped get you into this mess, so shouldn't they be willing to help the family get out?

♦ Sell household items that you no longer need or use. Consider eliminating at least one of your cars.

♦ Continue investing 10 percent of your income into your Automatic Investment Plan. This is your most important bill each month—it is the amount you owe to yourself and to your future.

♦ Send for a copy of your credit report. This will provide a good source for current information about your status, and how your creditors are rating you. It also gives you an opportunity to check for any mistakes.

To obtain the free copy you are entitled to once a year, send a written request to TRW Consumer Assistance, P.O. Box 2350, Chatsworth, California 91313. Include the following information:

- ◆ your first name, middle initial, and last name
- ◆ your spouse's first name
- ◆ your current address, verified by including a photo-copy of the name and address section of a recent utility or credit card bill
- ◆ Social Security number
- ◆ date of birth

For more information, contact TRW at 214-390-3000. You will receive the report in two or three weeks.

ACTIONS TO TAKE ON DAY 25

1. Call TRW (214-390-3000) and obtain your latest credit report.
2. If you are close to bankruptcy, negotiate with your creditors.
3. Set up a life-changing repayment plan.
4. Continue to invest in your AIP.

OBTAIN THE BEST FINANCIAL
INFORMATION FOR FREE!

This month we have reviewed the fundamental principles of sound money management. But this overview is not enough to keep you current with today's fast-changing markets. Events worldwide will affect your investments and require you to make adjustments to the funds you manage in your Automatic Investment Plan. You could stay informed by subscribing to dozens of different publications and by buying dozens of books, but these purchases would soon add up to hundreds of dollars. Subscribing to Value Line alone, one of the best sources for information on individual stocks, would cost over $500 per year.

Fortunately, you don't have to spend that much money to stay informed. Some of the best financial information in the world is available for no charge at all. You just have to know where to find it and, more important, what to look for when you get there. Today I'm going to tell you the answers to both these quests.

Local Public and University Libraries

Believe it or not, the local public or university library is at the top of the list. They subscribe to hundreds of publications, and they maintain back issues so you can search for earlier articles and track records. Unless you live in a retirement community, you will find most people are too busy to browse through libraries any more, so you have easy access to the periodicals and a quiet, pleasant atmosphere in which to read them. You might even make some new friends.

Almost every library carries the basics in investment literature. Check your library for the following:

♦ *Standard & Poor's Stock Guide*—provides a monthly update of over four thousand stocks, including utilities and preferred issues. This guide is good for learning basic financial information about the company if you know how to read the symbols. No written text, only numbers and notes.

♦ *Value Line Rating and Reports*—follows well-known highly liquid stocks listed on the major exchanges. Value Line provides background information, stock price, financial condition, and rank within its industry of listed stocks, including the company's name and address, all on one page. It has an excellent track record in rating individual stocks. Its #1-rated stocks have far outperformed the market averages.

♦ *OTC Stock Report*—provides basic information on over-the-counter (OTC) stocks. Similar to Value Line, but for the OTC market.

♦ *Economist*—international magazine that provides unique insight into the working of other countries, their financial systems, markets, and governments. Good reading and a must for international investing.

♦ *Forbes*—financial magazine with solid, often irreverent and hard-hitting reporting.

♦ *Wall Street Journal*—excellent source of news on daily financial activity in the U.S. markets.

♦ *Financial Times*—London-based source of excellent coverage of European markets. Adequate coverage of non-European markets.

♦ *Barrons*—weekly digest of financial information, owned by the same company that publishes the *Wall Street Journal*.

♦ *Morningstar Mutual Funds*—another good source of basic information about mutual funds. Ranks each mutual fund from one to five stars. Great one-page review of a fund and its history.

Investment Newsletters

Another great source for new financial information is the newsletter industry. The editors of newsletters are skilled at monitoring and dissecting current financial trends, bringing a unique personal perspective to their writings that is often missing from mainstream financial publications.

Hundreds of investment newsletters circulate in the United States. They cover a wide variety of topics ranging from complex options and commodities strategies to simple personal finance matters. The best ones investigate the cutting edge of new investment horizons and provide information unbiased by personal interest. Newsletters are expensive, of course, and it's difficult to know which to buy based on advertising alone.

Fortunately, you can sample these newsletters at no cost by calling the publishers and requesting sample copies of the letters. If it seems to fit your own investment philosophy, then subscribe to it. Most offer a ninety-day, money-back guarantee if you are not satisfied. Some even offer a full money-back guarantee for the whole term of the subscription.

One company, Select Information Exchange, will send you a catalog with a complete list of trial issue packages available. You can request a catalog by calling or writing Select Information Exchange, 244 W. 54th Street, Room 614, New York, New York 10019, 212-247-7123.

For a free sample copy of my monthly newsletter *Forecasts & Strategies*, write to:

Phillips Publishing International
7811 Montrose Road
Potomac, Maryland 20857
or call: 800-777-5005

If you would like to subcribe to *Forecasts & Strategies*, it is available to you at the special introductory price of $99.00. To order use the above 800 number or the special offer subscription card enclosed in this book.

ACTIONS TO TAKE ON DAY 26

1. Check your local public or university library for free financial information.
2. Send for a sample issue of my newsletter, *Forecasts & Strategies*, by calling Phillips Publishing Inc. at 800-777-5005 or 301-340-2100, or subscribe for a year at the special rate of $99.
3. Subscribe to the newsletters that fit your own investment philosophy.

GET YOUR LIFE IN ORDER

The activity scheduled for today demands careful attention. It won't take a lot of effort, but it does require you to consider an eventuality that most of us like to avoid thinking about. That eventuality, of course, is death. It happens to everyone, but because we don't like to think about it happening to us, we tend to put off preparing for it, often until it is too late.

There is nothing morbid about getting your estate organized properly. In fact, knowing that your estate will be distributed in the manner you choose will give you a greater sense of security than you expect.

Over the past month we have emphasized the importance of gaining control over your personal finances by:

♦   starting a consistent saving/investment plan

- getting a grip on your spending habits
- tracking your sources of income
- knowing the true value of all your assets and liabilities

But one thing you may still lack is a will! You need to make sure your estate and your family are secure, no matter what happens to you. On Day 11, we discussed the importance of having auto, medical, and life insurance and how to get the right amount of coverage at a reasonable price. Writing a will is simply another form of insurance, ensuring that your heirs will be protected after your death.

Millions of Americans die each year "intestate," or without a will. If you don't have a will, the state where you live will use its generic will to distribute your estate. Often that means giving your children two-thirds of your estate and your spouse only one-third. I don't know about your spouse, but my wife would be furious over such an arrangement. Even worse, if you and your spouse die at the same time leaving minor children, they will become wards of the state until a judge decides who should raise them. This provision alone should give you the incentive you need to start your will today.

A will can be very simple. You simply write a statement declaring who gets what when you die, have it notarized, and put it in a safe place where your heirs will find it. There are books available to tell you how to prepare your own will.

It is, however, safer and wiser to have a local attorney prepare a will for you. Most people need guidance on how to write it properly. An attorney will be familiar with the estate and probate laws of your state and will help you write a will that will satisfy both the state's requirements and your wishes.

Drawing up a simple will shouldn't cost much. Call your attorney if you have one, or check the Yellow Pages under attorneys and choose someone you and your pocketbook both feel comfortable with. Yes, there are discount lawyers, and a simple will need not cost hundreds of dollars. Shop around!

One More Suggestion

Another tip for married couples: If you haven't already done so, put your assets in joint ownership, so that you and your spouse both own your bank account, house, boat, investments, and other assets. Any asset you own individually will be probated, but joint ownership allows the surviving spouse to continue owning this asset without being frozen by the court. Of course, there may be legitimate reasons to maintain single ownership, such as children from a previous marriage, protecting assets from possible lawsuits, and so forth, but generally joint ownership is a good idea.

Living Trusts and Other Estate Planning Tools

There is much more to estate planning than simply writing a will. You may want to have an estate planner help you with other areas, so you can avoid probate and estate taxes as much as possible. Generally, I recommend estate planning beyond the writing of a simple will for anyone whose estate exceeds $250,000. Estate planning can help you

- ◆ avoid probate costs on your estate
- ◆ avoid federal and state taxes on estates and inheritances

Avoiding Probate

If your estate is complicated, perhaps involving several heirs, large holdings, and charitable beneficiaries, your property could be tied up for more than a year in court. Legal fees can mount up, swallowing as much as one-quarter of your estate!

Probate is the cause of these expensive delays. Your will must be probated in a court to transfer ownership from your estate to your heirs.

A living trust avoids probate because it continues living on after your death. You die technically penniless, while your trust, the owner of your assets, continues to live on. At the time of the owner's death, the executors of the estate follow the instructions of the trust and distribute the assets in a way the deceased wanted them to be distributed. No lengthy probate proceedings and expenses are involved.

Avoiding Estate Taxes

Larger estates worth more than $600,000 face federal and state taxes that can climb as high as 65 percent. Imagine your spouse losing over half your wealth just because you died. It's enough to make you sick to death!

Each person's estate is entitled to a $600,000 exemption before federal taxes apply. You can use this exemption during your lifetime or after death.

One technique to increase the exemption to $1.2 million is to split your estate into two parts—estate A, which contains $600,000 worth of assets, and estate B, the remainder of your estate. When you die, estate A goes to your heirs tax free, while estate B goes to your surviving spouse. Under current law, you can give any part of your estate to your surviving spouse without paying federal estate taxes. Then when your surviving spouse dies, the first $600,000 of the spouse's estate is exempt. Effectively, you have doubled the federal exemption to $1.2 million.

Life insurance is a common method of adding instant liquidity to your estate in order to pay federal taxes, which are due nine months after your death. The cheapest policies for this purpose are second-to-die term insurance. The insurance proceeds aren't paid to the estate until after the second spouse dies. As a result, annual premiums are extremely low, and cash is injected into the estate when federal taxes are due.

Finally, charitable trusts and foundations are a powerful way to eliminate federal estate liabilities entirely. You give part of your estate to your favorite church, alma mater, free-market think tank, or other charity or foundation. This is a great way to avoid all federal taxes—on income, capital gains, and estate! You can even set up your own private foundation to avoid taxes and benefit the world with another charitable cause.

Where to Go for Help

If your estate is large enough to consider these estate planning tools, I suggest you contact either of the following estate-planning organizations:

♦ David T. Phillips & Co., 3200 N. Dobson Road, Building C, Chandler, Arizona 85224, 800-223-9610, 602-897-6088.

♦ Wealth Transfer Planning Inc., 4225 Executive Square, Suite 300, LaJolla, California 92037, 800-423-4890, fax 619-658-7249.

Good luck!

ACTIONS TO TAKE ON DAY 27

1. Contact a local attorney, and write a will.
2. If appropriate, place your assets in joint ownership with your spouse.
3. Discuss a living trust and other estate planning tools with your attorney or financial advisor.
4. Plan ways to minimize estate taxes and probate by contacting a specialist.

REVIEW AND MEDITATION

This week has emphasized the need to be flexible and willing to accept change. Those who succeed are those who are willing to adapt to a changing situation, such as age, income, family status, and the state of the economy. Life is an adventure—be willing to explore new worlds!

Change Your Living Habits

Several years ago our family was enjoying a great deal of financial success, but we felt that our personal and intellectual lives were stagnating. We wanted to face new challenges and experience a new lifestyle. So we decided to pack up our family of four children and move to the Bahamas. We spent two wonderful years there. Yes, our children missed out on Little League, ballet lessons, Boy Scouts, and Brownies. They left behind their friends and familiar surroundings.

But they gained so much more than they lost! With no television, they spent hours reading, playing games with each other, and exploring the ocean in our backyard. We joined the Nassau Operatic Society and performed onstage in four musicals. Two of our children were hired as actors in a soft drink commercial, and our oldest daughter sang for the Queen of England. We spent idyllic days at Cabbage Beach and romantic nights listening to the waves splash against our sea wall. Best of all, we discovered where our true treasure lay—not in the things we had accumulated in our lifetime, but in the experiences we shared as a family.

Just as I encouraged you to evaluate your possessions to determine their true worth, we evaluated our possessions to determine what we must take with us and what we could do without. We discovered that there were indeed some things we missed: our books, our piano, our pictures. But we did not miss our television, our second car, our clothes dryer, or our exercise equipment. Most important, we discovered that we didn't want to live our lives as we had before, totally immersed in a business that provided lucrative income but also absorbed enormous amounts of our time and energy. By the time we returned from the Bahamas, we had changed our perspectives and our lives.

Interestingly, many of our friends in the financial world had been talking for some time about leaving the country and living an adventure, but none of them had the courage to do it until we did. There were too many things holding them back—business obligations, housing worries, community affairs, storing or discarding personal possessions, even the social pressure against making such an impetuous move. Yet when others did do it, they enjoyed marvelous experiences similar to ours. But it required a willingness to change and adapt.

This week we discussed the importance of being willing to change your attitude about assets, liabilities, spending, and debt. I encouraged you to evaluate your assets, weigh them against their liabilities, and eliminate those you no longer need, use, or value. Continue to streamline your life, eliminating those aspects of it you no longer value. You may be spending your time in community organizations, business associations, hobby clubs, or weekend activities simply because they have become a habit. If they no longer bring you satisfaction, cut them out of your life and put your time to better use. Change the way you spend your leisure time.

Exchange Passive Assets for Active Investments

Change the way you view your assets, too. Put passive assets to work for you by exchanging them for profit-yielding investments. We once owned a lovely piece of property overlooking a mountain in Utah. It was a great location—for someone who actually wanted to live in Utah. We did not. We bought it on speculation, expecting the price to rise. It did. Meanwhile, however, it generated no income and collected a number of liabilities, including property taxes, yard maintenance, and annoying phone calls from people who wanted to buy it. Finally we decided to sell and used that money to pay off a second mortgage on our house. In essence, paying off the loan was like garnering a 10.5 percent return on our investment property, in addition to the sizable capital gain. Some people criticized our decision, saying that the price would have risen even more if we had held on longer. Perhaps they are right—real estate does tend to rise over time. But we exchanged a passive asset that was costing us additional investment into a positive investment, earning money where we had been spending it.

Change Spending and Borrowing Habits

Perhaps the most important change you can make is in your spending and borrowing habits. This change will give you the freedom to make all the other changes, because it will liberate you from the debtors' prison that takes away your money, your energy, and your time. Change the way you approach problems. Too many people accept what others tell them is the right way to do things. Become a creative problem solver. Instead of asking, "What should I do?" ask, "What needs to be accomplished?" Then find alternatives other than spending money to solve problems of all sizes.

Embrace Change: A Great Story

Above all, be flexible! Don't think you are too old, or too set in your ways, or too tied up by responsibility to make any significant changes in your life.

A few years ago my wife and I wrote a book called *High Finance on a Low Budget*. As the typesetter keyed the book into her computer, she became more and more excited about the concept of money management we developed (and which I summarized in the earlier chapters of this book). One morning she told us, "We started last night! We are finally gaining control of our finances!"

At the time, she and her husband owned and operated a small graphic design company. They had three teenagers, and life was hectic. Money seemed to pour through their hands, and the debts were piling up. Although they worked extremely hard, they could see no relief in the future, and they were only one step ahead of the bill collectors. Almost at the point of having nothing left to lose, they decided to implement our plan for getting out of debt.

First they began writing down everything they spent every day. No longer could the kids come to them with a hand out, saying, "I need $35 for school" and expect Mom and Dad to fork over the dough. Now Mom's response was, "Why do you need this money?" followed by, "Is there a cheaper way we could do this?" Too often we accept people's demands as imperative and pay up without searching for alternatives.

Next, the entire family cut back on all activities and expenses except the bare essentials. This may seem drastic, especially for a family of teenagers involved in many worthwhile activities. How could we advocate the elimination of piano lessons? Children are only young once! Yet this family did it, and it worked. Instead of going to music lessons, crew practice, and dance lessons after school, the teens took part-time jobs, adding to the family finances instead of depleting them. The parents also looked for ways to supplement their income temporarily. Both were working long hard hours at the family business, but they decided that the wife should look for another job for a while, and the husband would simply double up his efforts at work. Because of her type-setting and bookkeeping skills, she was quickly hired as a secretary at a local business firm. Following our advice, they used all of her paycheck to pay down the debts that had been plaguing them for several years.

Six months later—yes, only six months later!—I saw my typeset-ter at a piano recital at which both her daughter and my daughter were performing. Their daughter was paying for half of her piano lessons with her part-time job. Their son was back on the crew team, but now he spearheaded fund raisers that he used to shun and helped reduce costs for the entire team. She had been promoted from secretary to office manager within weeks of starting work, and discovered that she loved working for her new boss. Meanwhile, her husband had discovered that by being more selective of the jobs and clients he accepted, he could run the graphics firm by himself, turn-ing a greater profit while working fewer hours.

In short, reading our book and applying its principles not only liberated them from debtors' prison, it gave them an entirely new approach to life. Everyone in the family was happier and more productive. With persistence and self-discipline, you can experi-ence a similar change in your own life.

ACTIONS TO TAKE ON DAY 28

1. Sit down and figure out how you would like to change to enjoy life more. Consider changing jobs, moving, a new hobby, or attending church.

2. Put all your assets to good use.

3. Change spending and borrowing habits—spend less, save more.

FIFTH WEEK:
Go on
Automatic Pilot

START A FINANCIAL LIBRARY

I love books. Over the years I have built quite an impressive collection, on topics ranging from economics and finance to religious studies and military biographies. I can't pass a bookstore without being pulled in by the lure of new ideas and old wisdom.

Today I am going to help you get started in building a millionaire's library. Over the years I've read and applied the principles of some outstanding financial works. All of them can be found in a bookstore or purchased through the mail. As you read them, you will gain insights that will help you improve your own money-making skills. These books are required reading for my students each semester in the investment course I teach at Rollins College.

The Richest Man in Babylon

Let me begin by recommending the greatest book ever written on personal finance, *The Richest Man in Babylon*, by George C. Clason. Clason wrote the book as a series of essays in the 1920s, and they have been popular ever since.

Clason begins his book by telling the story of Arkad, an ancient character who transforms himself from a poor chariot maker to the richest man in Babylon. His friends come to see him one day and ask him to reveal his secret. They note that they all started out at the same level and that Arkad appeared no better skilled in sport or intelligence than they. "Why, then, should a fickle fate single you out to enjoy all the good things of life and ignore us who are equally deserving?" they ask.

The remainder of the book is compilation of the fictional Arkad's stories as he reveals the simple secrets that helped him become so wealthy. Arkad sums it up neatly in one bold sentence: *"A part of all you earn is yours to keep."*

His friends laugh, thinking that everything they earn was theirs to keep, not just part of it. But Arkad explains that most if not all of their money goes to someone else: the baker, the sandal maker, the wine seller, the tax collector, and the landlord, for example. For most ordinary workers, nothing is left over, nothing is left for them to keep.

Arkad explains that early on, he made a commitment to save one-tenth of all his gross earnings. At first the sacrifice was difficult, he admits, especially when he watched his friends spending all their earnings. But soon saving became a habit and he no longer missed the money he saved.

The rest of the book shows how Arkad invested his savings wisely. At first he made mistakes and was swindled by some fraud peddlers because he blindly followed their advice. He gradually learned how business in Babylon functioned, and eventually he became a seasoned trader. He was so successful with his business that he became the richest man in Babylon.

Clason writes, "Far and wide he was famed for his wealth. Also he was famed for his liberality. He was generous in his charities. He was generous with his family. He was liberal in his own expenses. But nevertheless each year his wealth increased more rapidly than he spent it."

In many ways, the book you are reading right now is an updated version of *The Richest Man in Babylon*. Modern-day techniques, such as the Automatic Investment Plan (AIP) developed by discount brokerage firms, make it easy to implement Arkad's saving-investment plan. This book is Clason's plan made practical!

Note that no matter how generous or how much of a big spender Arkad was, he was always getting wealthier. The same principle applies to you—once you establish the AIP, you become richer every month no matter how much you take out of your checking account. That assumes, of course, that you don't borrow money to spend or give away. We've urged against excessive debt throughout this book.

How to order: Penguin Books, 375 Hudson Street, New York, New York 10014, $9.00.

How to Be Rich

My second favorite book is *How to Be Rich*, by J. Paul Getty. Getty wasn't very successful in marriage or family life, but he knew how to become rich.

Getty became the first billionaire in the world, and he did so by investing in the oil business. He started out as a wildcatter in Oklahoma in 1915. An independent operator in a high-risk business, Getty was never interested in joining the big oil companies. "Fortunes are being made—and lost—daily," he wrote. "It is not unusual for a penniless wildcatter, down to his last drill bit and without cash or credit, to drill another hundred feet and bring in a well that made him a rich man.... On the other hand, there were men who invested all they owned in leases and drilling operations only to find that they had nothing to show for their money and efforts but a few dismally dry holes. Leases purchased at peak prices one day proved to be utterly valueless the next."

Getty's lease proved lucky, and he was on the road to success. But it wasn't just luck that made him successful. Unlike the other wild-catters, who simply guessed at where a gusher might be found, Getty relied on geologists to find oil, an uncommon approach in those days.

Getty also bought oil stocks during the depths of the 1930s Depression, another unpopular move that proved shrewdly astute. Finally, in the 1940s, Getty bought oil concessions in the Middle East: "Instinct, hunch, luck—call it what you will," he said. "The Middle East was the most promising locale, the best bet, for oil exploration."

Getty understood the principles of hard work and thrift. His father didn't give money to his children until after they were old enough to earn a living. "A sense of thrift is essential for success in business. The businessman must discipline himself to practice economy whenever possible, in his personal life as well as his business affairs." Getty's motto was: "Make your money first—then think about spending it." Sound familiar? Regarding work, Getty wrote that even in his later life, "I still find it's often nec-essary to work 16 to 18 hours a day, and sometimes around the clock."

Like most successful investors, Getty believed in the funda-mental "bargain-hunting" approach to investing. "Get-rich-quick schemes just don't work," he said. "Making money in the stock market can't be done overnight or by haphazard buying and sell-ing. The big profits go to the intelligent, careful and patient investor, not to the reckless and overeager speculator." He recom-mended buying relatively low priced stocks in "industries that can-not help but burgeon as time goes on."

Getty was a strong believer in free enterprise. "Taxes are too high—and far too numerous. A logical, equitable tax program will have to be devised to replace the insane hodgepodge of federal, state, county, and city levies that make life a fiscal nightmare for everyone." Amen!

Getty also favored greater freedom in international trade.

"The long-term solution to our country's economic problems lies in more, not less, foreign trade."

How to order: Berkeley Order Department, P.O. Box 506, East Rutherford, New Jersey 07073, $4.95 paperback.

Grinding It Out

The best business book ever written is *Grinding It Out*, by Ray Kroc, the founder of McDonald's. Here's a man who started and became the leader in fast food restaurants at an age when most people are thinking of retiring. His autobiography tells the incredible story of a man driven by a desire to succeed. His rags-to-riches tale is a great example to anyone who wants to achieve financial independence. You can't put it down. Kroc describes in great detail what it takes to make a business succeed.

How to order: Contemporary Books Inc., 2 Presidential Plaza, Suite 1200, Chicago, Illinois 60601, $9.00 paperback.

One Up on Wall Street

Like the chapter on investing in J. Paul Getty's *How to Be Rich*, my next three book recommendations will help you become a better investor.

The first is *One Up on Wall Street*, by Peter Lynch, the #1 money manager of the 1980s. His Magellan Fund was the best performing mutual fund during the fifteen years he managed it. He quit in 1990 to spend more time with his family, although judging from his output since then, I wonder how much time he was able to spend at home.

Lynch knows how to make money. His book is full of examples of the "ten baggers," little-known growth companies that increase tenfold or more, usually after the institutional buyers discover them.

Lynch is the ultimate fundamentalist, looking for strong earnings, a solid balance sheet, and a relatively low price before he buys.

Can you beat the market and the pros, following Lynch's advice? Read the title again for the answer!

How to order: Penguin Books, 375 Hudson Street, New York, New York 10014, $10.95.

The Intelligent Investor

The second investment book I recommend is *The Intelligent Investor*, by Benjamin Graham, the father of security analysis. Warren Buffett, the richest man in America, says that Graham's book is "by far the best book on investing ever written." But bear in mind that this is a book for sophisticated investors who like to dig for facts and figures in company balance sheets. Graham studied company data constantly, looking for solid, blue-chip stocks that could be purchased at reasonable prices.

How to order: HarperCollins, 10 East 53rd Street, New York, New York 10022, $16.95.

Scrooge Investing

I hate to plug my own book, but the third recommendation for books on investments is my own: *Scrooge Investing*. It's now out in a second, updated edition, having sold over fifty thousand copies. The concept of becoming a Scrooge investor has been very well received. The Scrooge investor operates on three basic principles:

- ♦ Always look for bargain opportunities.

- ♦ Always be cost-conscious.

- ♦ Do your own homework.

Scrooge Investing adopts this philosophy for all areas of investing, with individual chapters on stocks, bonds, mutual funds, real estate, precious metals, currencies, and collectibles.

How to order: Dearborn Financial Publishing, 520 North Dearborn Street, Chicago, Illinois 60610, 800-322-8621, $19.95.

The Investor's Bible

If you are really interested in the whole area of investing, you might consider getting a copy of my textbook, *The Investor's Bible: Mark Skousen's Principles of Investment.* This 400-page, oversized workbook is used each semester in my course on investments at Rollins College. If you have a hard time understanding the world of high finance and all the various investment terms and products, you will find this textbook useful. The price is high, but that's because it covers the information contained in an entire college course.

How to order: Phillips Publishing, Inc., 7811 Montrose Road, Potomac, Maryland 20854, 800-777-5005, $195.

The Art of Contrary Thinking

Let me conclude by recommending a purely philosophical book, *The Art of Contrary Thinking*, by Humphrey B. Neill, the founder of contrarian thinking. Neill was an investment newsletter writer living in Vermont who liked to be alone with his thoughts. He liked to go against the crowd. "I find more and more that it is well to be on the side of the minority, since it is always the more intelligent," he once said.

But, to use contrarian thinking in the investment world is easier said than done, according to Neill. "The public is right *during* the trends, but wrong at both ends!" How does one know when the trend has changed? Ah, there's the rub. It's more an art than a science.

How to order: Contrary Opinion Library, Fraser Publishing Co., Box 494, Burlington, Vermont 05420, 802-658-0322, $9.95.

Conclusion

Well-researched financial books written by seasoned investors are the best source of information today. They should form the foundation for your daily, weekly, or monthly publications. Start your collection today.

ACTIONS TO TAKE ON DAY 29

1. Begin a financial library.
2. Obtain some or all of the books recommended in this chapter.
3. Use the information to help you make wise investment decisions.

CELEBRATE YOUR
FINANCIAL INDEPENDENCE

You've made it! It has been one month since you started on the road to financial independence.

When you first picked up the book, you were probably skeptical of its claims. Thirty days to being independently wealthy?

Yet, if you have followed the day-to-day checklist, you *are* on the road to financial independence. You are building an independent source of wealth that can't help but burgeon over time. You are reducing your wasteful expenditures and increasing your income. You are cutting out consumer debt and building your net worth. Eventually you will achieve that lofty goal of complete independence and security.

An Upside-down World

You must always be alert to a *false* sense of independence and security. Last week I saw a little pamphlet in a bank: "Live as if you're independently wealthy." Curious, I read it. The pamphlet went on: "Whether you have a sudden urge to travel, or you have long-anticipated expenses to cover...

"...A Home Equity Creditline lets you write yourself a loan anytime."

Notice that the bank never uses the word DEBT in its advertisement for a home-equity loan. As I wrote earlier, only in the world of retail is a debt called credit, spending called saving, and consumer goods called investments. You must guard against false images of wealth. Debt and liabilities are not wealth, saving and assets are.

Our Plan of Action: First Things First!

Notice our approach throughout this book. First, we established the most important action to take—start a saving/investment program now, and make it easy to save/invest through an Automatic Investment Plan (AIP). Yes, start saving/investing now, *before* you do anything else. Before you get out of debt, reduce your wasteful expenditures, sell off unproductive assets, make a will, or buy that used car. Joining an AIP is the first and foremost action to take in order to become financially independent. It is the linchpin of monetary success.

We recommended that you invest at least 10 percent of your take-home pay in your AIP. If you can put in more, great, you'll achieve your objectives faster. I know some individuals who save 30 percent each paycheck.

Naturally, this investment program will squeeze your budget and your lifestyle. That's what it's supposed to do—put pressure on you each month to keep your expenses low, stay out of consumer debt, and establish discipline in your financial affairs.

Wasting Money

The second week was spent on various ways to cut out waste. You may have noticed that, of all the weeks, this one contained the most material. Our main point was that everyone, rich and poor, wastes money. At least 10 percent of your income is wasted on food, entertainment, housing, transportation, insurance, and so forth. You may not know where the waste is. We don't either. But you *are* wasting money!

By using the techniques outlined in Week 2, you should be able to pinpoint the areas where you can cut back without reducing your standard of living. You may be eating out too much. You may be paying too much for insurance.

You may be wasting your money buying lottery tickets or other forms of gambling. Or your car or house payments may be out of line with your income. By listing all your expenditures for a month or two, you will discover an amazing amount of wasteful spending. It's time to cut out the fat.

When I lived in Latin America and the Caribbean, I was amazed at how well people can live on low budgets, far below those of the average American. Somehow, they were able to live in a house, own a car, television, and other conveniences, all on an income a tenth of the average American. And without using credit cards.

Don't tell me Americans aren't wasting money.

Increasing Your Income

The third week was devoted to ways of increasing your income at work and in your investment portfolio. Strangely, most Americans think that a lack of income is the source of all their financial woes, so why did we wait until the third week to discuss it? Shouldn't it have been the first week, the first day?

No! Getting more income does not automatically solve your financial problems. Even millionaires get into trouble. You must first get hold of your expense account. Discipline and thrift are the key principles you must learn first, and therefore we have put discipline and thrift ahead of income in importance.

Once you have established the virtues of discipline and thrift, earning more income will increase your net worth. We showed you the time-tested methods of increasing your income: getting a raise by being more productive at work; starting your own business; and investing wisely in other peoples' businesses, i.e., the stock market.

Selling Off Your Unproductive Assets

In the fourth week, we concentrated on your assets and liabilities. We suggested ways to increase the productivity of your estate by selling off unproductive assets and putting the proceeds into your investment account. The key to financial independence is to build your investment account as quickly as possible. You do this by:

♦ investing automatically every month

♦ selling off unproductive assets and placing the funds in your investment account

♦ increasing your automatic investing each month as your income increases

♦ reducing your debts, so as to have more funds to save/invest

♦ investing unexpected bonuses, gifts, and such—not spending money, but investing it—a penny saved is a penny earned!

Avoid Consumer Debt

One of the biggest stumbling blocks on your way to achieving financial independence is "easy credit." Having a credit card handy at the shopping mall and lately even at the convenience store is an open invitation to waste and financial ruin. It always shocks me to see how many people pull out their credit card to buy food at Wendy's or 7-Eleven!

My advice: get rid of your credit cards. Get a debit card from Visa or MasterCard, which looks just like a credit card except that the money is taken out of your checking account immediately to pay the bill. This blocks paying off your expenditures over months or years at high interest charges.

Refinance your mortgage and take advantage of lower interest rates. Avoid financing a new car purchase. Don't buy a new car— buy a two- or three-year-old used car. Finance it only if you can't pay for it with cash.

Get Your Estate in Order

Finally, get your house in order. Arrange for a legally binding will through a local attorney. If your estate is large enough, consider establishing trusts and other options to avoid probate and federal estate taxes.

Everything Is on "Automatic" Now

If you have followed through on the checklist you were given each day, you should now be on "automatic pilot," destined to achieve financial independence. The AIP will increase your net worth each year, no matter how much you spend. The No-Budget Budget (writing down all your daily expenses) will cut your wasteful expenditures to the bone. A debit card will force you to avoid high interest charges on your credit card. And a will will give you peace of mind.

Congratulations! You've solved all your major financial problems in one month. While the rest of the your friends, neighbors, business acquaintances, and relatives struggle to make ends meet, you can think about more enjoyable things in life.

It's Time to Celebrate

Having done all these things, you deserve a reward.

Remember Day 1? We recommended that you take the day off and contemplate how the next thirty days would be very different from the previous days of your life. We suggested you take a one-day vacation at the beach, a park, or another relaxing location and plan your next month's activities according to the instructions in this book.

You may have started the month thinking everything was hopeless. You may have been working full time and seemingly making no headway. You may have been deeply in debt. You may have been unhappy about your finances or have lost money in the stock market or in a bad investment deal. Whatever your circumstances, this book has renewed in you a sense of hope.

On Day 30, we recommend you reward yourself by going out for the evening. Go out to dinner with your spouse and family. Go out dancing. Go bowling. Relax and enjoy yourself. You are on the road to financial independence.

Just remember one thing: Be sure to pay in cash!

ACTIONS TO TAKE ON DAY 30

Having followed the checklist throughout this book, you are on "Automatic Pilot," flying directly toward financial independence. To celebrate, take the night off and go out to dinner, go dancing, and enjoy yourself. And pay for it in cash!

TOOLS FOR THE
FINANCIALLY INDEPENDENT

DISCOUNT BROKERS

For your AIP or Mutual Funds

Charles Schwab & Co., Inc.
101 Montgomery St.
San Francisco, CA 94120-0332
for Mutual Funds/AIP: 800-526-8600
for IRAs: 800-435-4000

Fidelity Funds Network
P.O. Box 660306
Dallas, TX 75266
800-544-9697

Jack White & Co.
Towne Centre Dr., Suite 220
San Diego, CA 92122
800-233-3411

Other General Discount Brokers

Kennedy Cabot
9470 Wilshire Blvd.
Beverly Hills, CA 90212
800-252-0090

Quick & Reilly
26 Broadway 11th Fl.
New York, NY 10004-1899
800-926-0600

SUGGESTED READING

The Art of Contrary Thinking
by Humphrey B. Neill
Contrary Opinion Library
Fraser Publishing Co.
P.O. Box 494
Burlington, VT 05420
802-658-0322

Charles Allmon's Growth Stock Advisory
4405 East-West Highway, Suite 305
Bethesda, MD 20814
800-742-5476

***Entrepreneur* magazine**
2392 Morse Ave.
Irvine, CA 92714
714-261-2325

Grinding It Out
by Ray Kroc
Contemporary Books Inc.
2 Presidential Plaza, Suite 200
Chicago, IL 60601

***How I Turned $1,000 into $1,000,000 in Real Estate—
In My Spare Time***
by Bill Nickerson
Simon & Schuster Trade Division
1230 Avenue of the Americas
New York, NY 10020
212-698-7000

How To Be Rich
by J. Paul Getty
Berkeley Order Department
P.O. Box 506
East Rutherford, NJ 07073

Inc. **magazine**
38 Commercial Wharf
Boston, MA 02110-3883
617-248-8000

The Intelligent Investor
by Benjamin Graham
HarperCollins
10 East 53rd St.
New York, NY 10022

**The Investor's Bible: Mark Skousen's
Principles of Investment**
by Mark Skousen
Phillips Publishing International
7811 Montrose Rd.
Potomac, MD 20854
800-777-5005

Mark Skousen's *Forecasts & Strategies*
Phillips Publishing International
7811 Montrose Rd.
Potomac, MD 20854
800-777-5005

Morningstar **Inc.**
225 West Wacker Dr.
Chicago, IL 60606
800-876-5005

One Up on Wall Street
by Peter Lynch
Penguin Books
375 Hudson St.
New York, NY 10014

The Richest Man in Babylon
by George C. Clason
Penguin Books
375 Hudson St.
New York, NY 10014

Scrooge Investing
by Mark Skousen
Dearborn Financial Publishing
520 North Dearborn St.
Chicago, IL 60610
800-322-8621

Standard and Poor's Stock Guide
at your local library

Taipan
Agora Publishing Inc.
826 E. Baltimore St.
Baltimore, MD 21202

Value Line Investment Survey
at your local library

For the world's largest selection of free market books, contact:

Laissez Faire Books
938 Howard St., #202
San Fransisco, CA 94103
to order, or for a free catalog, call 800-326-0996

For your health

Dr. Marcus Laux's *Malibu Natural Health Letter*
Earl Mindell's *Joy of Health*
Julian Whitaker's *Health & Healing*
all through:
Phillips Publishing International
7811 Montrose Rd.
Potomac, MD 20854
800-777-5005

BUSINESS ADVICE, CREDIT INFORMATION

Better Business Bureau
contact your local chapter

Federal Trade Commission's Consumer Protection Bureau
Credit Practices Division
Washington, DC 20580
202-326-2222

International Franchise Association
1350 New York Ave. NW, Suite 900
Washington, DC 20005
800-543-1038

SCORE
409 3rd St. SW, 4th floor
Washington, D.C. 20024
202-205-6762

TRW Consumer Assistance
P.O. Box 2350
Chatsworth, CA 91313
214-390-3000

ESTATE PLANNING

David T. Phillips & Co.
3200 N. Dobson Rd., Building C
Chandler, AZ 85224
800-223-9610

Wealth Transfer Planning Inc.
4225 Executive Square, Suite 300
LaJolla, CA 92037
800-423-4890

FIVE LOW RATE CREDIT CARDS

Arkansas Federal Credit Card Services
1515 Merrill Dr., Suite 200
Little Rock, AR 72211
800-477-3348

Oak Brook Bank
1400 W. 16th St.
Oak Brook, IL 60521
800-666-1011

Peoples Bank of Bridgeport
850 Main St.
Bridgeport, CT 06601
800-423-3273

Simmons First National Bank
P.O. Box 7009
Pine Bluff, AR 71611
800-636-5151

Wachovia
P.O. Box 15145
Wilmington, DE 19886-5145
800-842-3262

INSURANCE

David T. Phillips & Co.
N. Dobson Rd., Building C
Chandler, AZ 85224
800-223-9610
602-897-6088

GEICO
One GEICO Plaza
Washington, DC 20076
800-824-5404

USAA
9800 Fredericksburg Rd.
San Antonio, TX 78288
800-531-8319

ONLINE COMPUTER SERVICES & SOFTWARE FOR BUDGETING

America On-line
8619 Westwood Center Dr., Suite 200
Vienna, VA 22182
800-827-6364

CompuServe
P.O. Box 20212
Columbus, OH 43220
800-848-8990

GEnie
401 N. Washington St.
Rockville, MD 20849
800-638-9636

Prodigy
445 Hamilton Ave.
White Plains, NY 10601
800-776-3449

Quicken
2650 E. Elvira St.
Tuscon, AZ 85706-7123

TO REMOVE YOUR NAME FROM MOST MAILING LISTS

Direct Marketing Association
1120 Avenue of the Americas
New York, NY 10036
212-768-7277

BUYING A CAR

EG & G Dynatrend
2300 Clarendon Blvd., Suite 705
Attn. PAL
Arlington, VA 22201

National Automobile Dealers Association (NADA) Blue Book
8400 Westpark Dr.
McLean, VA 22102
800-544-6232

Nationwide Auto Brokers
17517 West Ten Mile Rd.
Southfield, MI 48075
800-521-7257

FORECLOSURE INFORMATION

Fannie Mae
Foreclosures
1 North Charles St., Suite 1503
Baltimore, MD 21201

Resolution Trust Corporation
P.O. Box 44259
Jacksonville, FL 32231-4259
800-782-3006

ABOUT THE AUTHOR

Mark Skousen has been editor-in-chief of *Forecasts & Strategies* for the past fifteen years. It is now one of the largest investment newsletters in the United States, with over fifty thousand subscribers.

In addition to writing his investment letter, Dr. Skousen is an adjunct professor of economics and finance at Rollins College, Department of Economics, Winter Park, Florida 32789, and an occasional contributor to *Forbes, Reason, Human Events*, and *Liberty* magazines. He writes a monthly column for *The Freeman* entitled "Correction, Please!" published by the Foundation for Economic Education, Irvington on Hudson, New York 10533.

Dr. Skousen has authored fifteen books. His financial bestsellers include *High Finance on a Low Budget* (co-authored with his wife, Jo Ann), *The Complete Guide to Financial Privacy*, and *Scrooge Investing*. His latest work is *The Investor's Bible: Mark Skousen's Principles of Investment*. His economics books include *Economics on Trial, The Structure of Production*, and *Dissent on Keynes*. Skousen is a former economic analyst for the Central Intelligence Agency and has a Ph.D. in economics from George Washington University.

For more information on his newsletter and books, contact Phillips Publishing, Inc., at 800-777-5005.

INDEX